D1431293

A BEIRUT ANTHOLOGY

A BEIRUT ANTHOLOGY

Travel Writing
through the Centuries

Edited by
T.J. Gorton

The American University in Cairo Press
Cairo   New York

Copyright © 2015 by
The American University in Cairo Press
113 Sharia Kasr el Aini, Cairo, Egypt
420 Fifth Avenue, New York, NY 10018
www.aucpress.com

Exclusive distribution outside Egypt and North America by I.B.Tauris & Co Ltd.,
6 Salem Road, London, W2 4BU

Dar el Kutub No. 13828/14
ISBN 978 977 416 698 3

Dar el Kutub Cataloging-in-Publication Data

Gorton, Ted
        A Beirut Anthology/ T.J. Gorton.—Cairo: The American University
in Cairo Press, 2015.
                p.   cm.
                1.   ISBN 978 977 416 698 3
        Beirut (Lebanon) —description & travel
        915.6925

1 2 3 4 5   19 18 17 16 15

Designed by Fatiha Bouzidi
Printed in Egypt

Contents

Introduction

This city is one of those that must live and relive, come what may; the conquerors pass on and the city is reborn behind them. —Elisée Reclus, *L'Homme et la Terre*

Beirut is indeed an elusive city—a moving target that is liable to be transformed, to have moved on by the time you reach it. If not all things, it is many things to many people: the Orient  to the curious westerner, the West to the insular Middle Easterner. A palimpsest where history's moving finger has done a lot of writing, and a lot of moving on, neglecting to scrape the vellum clean after each chapter. A place of contrast: fleshpots and vice; education, scholarship and publishing; commerce and money and innovation; creative and constructive when it is not shady or worse. A place of intrigue and conspiracy, where the political dirty linen of a violent neighborhood comes to be washed. A place in Asia where you can get a real American hamburger or a proper *tournedos Rossini* as easily as an amazing variety of delicious local dishes. A place where, sadly, fifty years of untrammeled development, chaotic construction, and a brutal civil war have largely blighted a location of what was uniquely stunning natural beauty. And which, despite it all, stubbornly retains its charm and somehow both captivates and repels the new arrival.

The Canaanites, Egyptians, Assyrians, Seleucids, Romans, Persians, Arabs, Crusaders, Arabs again, Turks, French, everybody has conquered it and stayed a few months or many centuries. There are vestiges of all that, but they do not leap out at you unbidden as they do in Cairo: the visitor has to look for them, to work for the satisfaction of acquiring a sense of historical narrative lurking behind the clutter, bustle, and din of the modern city. Many of the monuments described by travelers from the eighteenth and nineteenth centuries no longer exist. Fortunately, the city that was, scraps of which do still exist, was an unmissable stop—often the first—on the Grand Tour or a pilgrimage to the Holy Land, and every tourist or pilgrim left a record of his or her travels. The dynamism of the people, the medley of languages and cultures and religions and world-views that coexist there, more or less comfortably, have not changed. The result is a uniquely atmospheric and volatile mix that some people hate, others find addictive, but no one reacts to with indifference.

Note: In antiquity, and indeed in many sources written before the Lebanese Republic was created in 1943, Beirut is described as being in "Syria," which referred not to the territory of the modern state of that name, but to a wide geographical area covering much of today's Syria, Lebanon, and part of Jordan.

Berytus, Mother of Laws

Berytus, always an important commercial center, became the foremost center for legal scholarship in the later Roman Empire, ahead of Constantinople and Alexandria. It had begun to decline, along with the Empire itself, when it was destroyed by a deadly earthquake in 551, from which it took centuries to recover.

Historical Survey, 1858
Murray's Handbook

Beyrout, or as it is sometime written Beirut, occupies the site, as it preserves the name, of the Berytus of the Greeks and Romans. It was probably founded by the Phoenicians, though the first mention of it is in the writings of Strabo, and the first historical notice only extends back as far as the year B.C. 140, when it was destroyed by Tryphon, the usurper of the throne of Syria, during the reign of Demetrius Nicator. After its capture by the Romans it was colonized by veterans of the Fifth Macedonian and Eighth Augustan Legions, and called "Colonia Julia Augusta Felix Berytus." It was here that Herod the Great procured the flagitious mock trial to be held over his two sons. The elder Agrippa greatly favoured the city, and adorned it with a splendid theatre and amphitheatre, besides baths and porticos, inaugurating them with games and spectacles of every kind, including shows of gladiators. Here, too after the destruction of Jerusalem, Titus celebrated the birthday of his father Vespasian by the exhibition of similar spectacles, in which many of the captive Jews perished.

But it was chiefly as a seat of learning that ancient Beyrout was celebrated. Its fame drew to it students from distant countries. Law, philosophy, and languages were cultivated. The well-known Gregory Thaumaturgus, after passing through Athens and Alexandria, came here to complete his knowledge of civil law; and Appion the martyr spent a time at Beyrout engaged in the study of Greek literature. From the 3rd to the 6th centy. was the golden age of Beyrout's literary history. In A.D. 551 the town was laid in ruins by an earthquake, and its learned men sought a temporary asylum at Sidon. . . . In the year 1110 Beyrout was captured by the crusaders under Baldwin I; it remained long in their hands, was made the seat of a Latin bishop, and was celebrated, as it is still, for the richness and beauty of its gardens and orchards. With the exception of a short occupation by Saladin the Christians retained possession of the town until the final overthrow of their power in 1291.

Foundation Myth, c. AD 450
Nonnus of Panopolis

Nonnus refers to the myth that Beroë (Beirut) was founded by Kronos, father of Zeus, at a very early phase in the Greek cosmogony.

Come now, ye Muses of Lebanon on the neighbouring land of Beroë, that handmaiden of Law! . . . There is a city Beroë, the keel of human life, harbour of the Loves, firm-based on the sea with fine islands and fine verdure, with a ridge of isthmus narrow and long, where the rising neck between two seas is beaten by the waves of both. On one side it spreads under the deep-wooded ridge of Assyrian Lebanon in the blazing East. . . . O Beroë, root of life, nurse of cities, the boast of princes, the first city seen, twin sister of Time, coeval with the universe, seat of Hermes, land of justice, land of laws, abode of Euphrosyne, house of [*Aphrodite of Paphos*], hall of the lovers, star of the Lebanon country. . . . Beroë came the first, coeval with the universe her agemate, bearing the name

of the nymph later born, which the colonizing sons of
. . . Rome shall call Berytos, since here fell a neighbour
to Lebanon.

A Difficult Neighborhood, c. AD 18
Strabo

Now all the mountainous parts are held by Ituraeans and
Arabians, all of whom are robbers, but the people in the
plains are farmers; and when the latter are harassed by
the robbers at different times they require different kinds
of help. These robbers use strongholds as bases of operation; those, for example, who hold Libanus possess, high
up on the mountain, Sinna and Borrama and other for-
tresses like them, and, down below, Botrys and Gigartus
and the caves by the sea and the castle that was erected
on Theuprosopon. Pompey destroyed both these places;
and from them the robbers overran both Byblus and the
city that comes next after Byblus, I mean the city Berytus, which lie between Sidon and Theuprosopon.

But though Berytus was razed to the ground by Tryphon, it has now been restored by the Romans; and it

received two legions, which were settled there by Agrippa, who also added to it much of the territory of Massyas, as far as the sources of the Orontes River. These sources are near Mt. Libanus and Paradeisus and the Aegyptian fortress situated in the neighbourhood of the land of the Apameians. So much, then, for the places on the sea.

Favorite of Agrippa, AD 94
Flavius Josephus

Now as Agrippa [I] was a great builder in many places, he paid a peculiar regard to the people of Berytus; for he erected a theater for them, superior to many others of that sort, both in sumptuousness and elegance, as also an amphitheater, built at vast expenses; and besides these, he built them baths and porticoes, and spared for no costs in any of his edifices, to render them both handsome and large. He also spent a great deal upon their dedication, and exhibited shows upon them, and brought thither musicians of all sorts, and such as made the most delightful music of the greatest variety. He also showed his magnificence upon the theater, in his great number of gladiators; and there it was that he exhibited the several antagonists, in order to please the spectators; no fewer indeed than seven hundred men to fight with seven hundred other men and allotted all the malefactors he had for this exercise, that both the malefactors might receive their punishment, and that this operation of war might be a recreation in peace. And thus were these criminals all destroyed at once.

Desolation, c. AD 555
Joannes Barbucallus

Here I lie, the luckless city, no longer a city, with my dead inhabitants, most ill-fated of all towns. After the Earth-shaker's shock Hephaestus consumed me. Alas, how excellent my beauty who now am dust!

Do ye who pass me by bewail my fate and shed a tear in honour of Berytus that is no more. Where is Cypris, the keeper of the city, that she may see her who was once the seat of the Graces become the dwelling-place of spectres? The city is the tomb of dead men who had no funeral; under her ashes we, Beroë's many thousands,

rest. . . . Inscribe upon a single stone above us, dear mortals who survive: "Here lies Berytus, lamented city, buried above ground. Sailor, stay not thy vessel's course for me, nor lower thy sails, dry land is the port you see. I am become one tomb. Let some other place that knows not mourning hear the beat of thine oars as thy ship approaches. This is Poseidon's pleasure and that of the Hospitable gods. Farewell seafarers, farewell wayfarers!"

Crusader Times

One after the other, the cities of the Levant fell to the Christian armies that invaded in the late eleventh century, seeking to recover Jerusalem for the Cross and to carve out kingdoms and fortunes for themselves in the process. This openly sectarian conflict left a deep imprint on the mentality of the region.

Ruins and Columns, 1052
Nasir-i-Khusrau

The renowned Persian traveler and scholar Nasir-i-Khusrau gives a description of the city about fifty years before the invasion of crusading Christian armies began a two-century Levantine historical hiatus.

From Jubail we came on to Bairut. Here I saw an arch of stone so great that the roadway went out through it; and the height of the arch I estimated at fifty ells (Gez). The side walls of the arch are built of white stone, and each block must be over a thousand Manns (or about a ton and a half) in weight. The main building is of unburnt brick, built up a score of ells high. Along the top of the same are set marble columns, each eight ells tall, and so thick that with difficulty could two men with their arms stretched embrace the circumference. Above these columns they have built arcades, both to right and to left, all of stones, exactly fitted, and constructed without mortar or cement. The great centre arch rises up between, and towers above the arcades by a height of fifty cubits. The blocks of stone that are used in the construction of these arches, according to my estimate, were each eight cubits high and four cubits across, and by conjecture each must weigh some seven thousand Manns (or about ten tons). Every one of these stones is beautifully fashioned and sculptured after a manner that is rarely accomplished, even in (soft) wood.

Except this arch no other (ancient) building remains. I inquired in the neighbourhood what might have been the purpose thereof; to which the people answered that, as they had heard tell, this was the Gate of Pharaoh's garden; also that it was extremely ancient. All the plain around this spot is covered with marble columns, with their capitals and shafts. These were all of marble, and chiselled, round, square, hexagonal, or octagonal; and all in such extremely hard stone that an iron tool can make no impression on it. Now, in all the country round there is apparently no mountain or quarry from which this stone can have been brought; and, again, there is another kind of stone that has an appearance of being artificial, and, like the first stone, this, too, is not workable with iron. In various parts of Syria there may be seen some five hundred thousand columns, or capitals and shafts of columns, of which no one now knows either the maker, or can say for what purpose they were hewn, or whence they were brought.

The Fall of Beirut, 1111
William of Tyre

An eyewitness account of one of Beirut's many sieges, beginning one of its many foreign occupations.

King Baldwin . . . gathered all the forces of his kingdom and laid siege to the city of Beirut. . . . Nearby the city there was a fine pine grove which was called the Pineda; this was most useful to our side, for they used the wood to make siege engines such as catapults and trebuchets and mangonels and ladders, all of which operated day and night and so caused great damage to those inside the walls.

Thus the siege continued for two whole months, and the long delay began to weigh on the besiegers. They therefore threw themselves into the attack even more fiercely than usual; those on the wooden towers could see that the inhabitants were desperate and sorely frightened. The towers were brought up to the walls and soldiers began to climb onto the battlements. Finally there were so many of our men inside that they managed to open one of the city gates, and the remainder of the army surged in. The Turks in the city fled towards the sea, thinking to escape that way; but our men in the galleys met them most cruelly with swords and forced them back. Finally after so many of them had been killed that the streets were running with blood, the survivors cried out for mercy to the King, that they should be spared. The King took pity on them and forbade his army from killing any more of them. Thus the city of Beirut was taken in the Year of Our Lord 1111, on the 27th day of April.

A Border Town, 1177
Johannes Phocas

By the time the Greek priest–pilgrim Phocas reached Beirut, the Crusaders controlled the Levant from Antioch to the coast of Syria–Lebanon and Palestine, with Jerusalem as centerpiece.

. . . and then comes Berytus, a large and populous city, set round about with spacious meadows, and adorned with a fair harbour. The harbour is not a natural one, but has been wrought by art, and is embosomed in the city in the form of a half-moon, and at the two extremities of the half-moon are placed, as horns, two great towers, from one of which a chain is drawn across to the other, and shuts in the ships within the harbour. This place is on the border between Syria and Phoenicia.

To the Holy Land

The Mamluks followed up the victories of the great Kurdish general Saladin to evict the last Crusader holdouts in 1291. There were not many European pilgrims and certainly no tourists for a few centuries, but by the mid-sixteenth century, it was possible for hardy voyagers to come in either guise.

European Discovery of Bananas, 1548
Antoine Regnault

We continued on our way and came to Beirut, a sea port where our Dragoman made us get down and walk. The Saracens call us Chamupcaour, which means "dirty Christian;" that is because they wash their feet, hands and face as often as possible. Christians do not perform any such ablutions. From there we proceeded to a small Monastery of Maronite Christians, in which there were two monks of the minor orders, and two converts living according to the Roman Church; they told us they were from the convent of Saint Francis on Mount Zion, in the province of Jerusalem.

In the environs of Beirut, the countryside is adorned with fruit trees, including sebesten [cordia], fig-trees, orange-trees, olive-trees, and pomegranates. There is also a small fruit grown there, like a cucumber, which is as sweet as sugar, and which they call Adam's apple; its leaves are six feet long.

Arrival in Beirut, 1697
Henry Maundrell

The Antonine way extends about a quarter of an hour's travel. It is at present so broken and uneven, that to repair it would require no less labour, than that wherewith it was at first made.

After this pass, you come upon a smooth sandy shore, which brings you, in about one hour and a half, to the river Beroot (for I could learn no other name it had). It is a large river, and has over it a stone bridge of six arches. On its other side is a plain field near the sea, which is said to be the stage on which St. George duell'd and kill'd the dragon. In memory of this atchievement, there is a small chappel built upon the place, dedicated at first to that Christian hero; but now perverted to a mosque. From hence, in an hour, we arrived at Beroot, very wet . . . .

The day following we spent at Beroot; being credibly inform'd that the river Damer, which lay in our next stage, was so swoln by the late rains that it would be impassable. This place was call'd anciently Berytus; from which the idol Baal Berith is supposed to have got its name. And afterwards being greatly esteemed by Augustus, had many privileges conferr'd upon it: and together with a new name, viz. Julia Felix. But at present, it retains nothing of its ancient felicity, except the situation; and that in particular is indeed very happy. It is seated on the sea-side, in a soil fertile and delightful, rais'd only so high above the salt water, as to be secure from its overflowings, and all other noxious and unwholesome effects of that element. It has the benefits of good fresh springs flowing down to it from the adjacent hills, and dispensed all over the city, in convenient and not unhandsome fountains. But besides these advantages of its situation, it has at present nothing else to boast of.

The Ottoman City

Beirut was always its own kind of city, an unholy mix of religion, learning, commerce, and vice. It stood out from other cities of the later Ottoman Empire, being more international (meaning more Europeanized) than most. Only the great cosmopolitan cities, Alexandria and Smyrna, surpassed it in that: but Beirut was different, in that its own 'native' population (itself quite diverse) became at least superficially cosmopolitan.

Palace of Fakhr al-Din, 1697
Henry Maundrell

The emir Faccardine had his chief residence in this place. He was in the reign of the sultan Morat, the fourth emir, or prince of the Druses; a people suppos'd to have descended from some dispers'd remainders of those christian armies, that engaged in the crusades, for the recovery of the Holy-Land: who afterwards, being totally routed, and despairing of a return to their native country again, betook themselves to the mountains hereabout; in which their descendants have continued ever since. . . .

We went to view the palace of this prince, which stands on the north east part of the city. At the entrance of it is a marble fountain, of greater beauty than is usually seen in Turkey. The palace within consists of several courts, all now run much to ruin; or rather perhaps never finish'd. The stables, yards for horses, dens for lions and other salvage creatures, gardens, &c. are such as would not be unworthy of the quality of a prince in Christendom, were they wrought up to that perfection of which they are capable, and to which they seem to have been design'd by their first contriver.

But the best sight that this palace affords, and the worthiest to be remember'd, is the orange garden. It contains a large quadrangular plat of ground, divided into sixteen lesser squares, four in a row, with walks between them. The walks are shaded with orange trees, of a large spreading size, and all of so fine a growth both for stem and head, that one cannot imagine any thing more perfect in this kind. . . .

On the east side of this garden were two terrace walks rising one above the other, each of them having an ascent to it of twelve steps. They had both several fine spreading orange trees upon them, to make shades in proper places. And at the north end they led into booths, and summer-houses, and other apartments very delightful, this place being design'd by Faccardine for the chief seat of his pleasure. It may perhaps be wonder'd, how this emir should be able to contrive any thing so elegant and regular as this garden; seeing the Turkish gardens are usually nothing else but a confus'd miscellany of trees, jumbled together without either knots, walks, arbours, or any thing of art or design, so that they seem like thickets rather than gardens; but Faccardine had been in Italy, where he had seen things of another nature, and knew well how to copy them in his own country. For indeed it appears by these remains of him, that he must need have been a man much above the ordinary level of a Turkish genius.

In another garden we saw several pedestals for statues; from whence it may be inferr'd, that this emir was no very zealous mahometan. At one corner of the same garden stood a tower of about sixty foot high; design'd to have been carried to a much greater elevation for a watchtower, and for that end built with an extraordinary strength, its walls being twelve foot thick.

We saw many granite pillars and remnants of mosaick floors; and in an heap of rubbish, several pieces of polish'd marble, fragments of statues, and other poor relicks of this city's ancient magnificence. On the sea side is an old ruin'd castle, and some remains of a small mole.

Misery and Splendor, 1665
Laurent d'Arvieux

The city of Beirut is dark, its streets narrow and filthy. It is quite populous, most of its inhabitants being Greek Christians and Maronites. . . . The rest are Moors, Turks, or Jews; they are all laborers or artisans. Beirut's commerce is substantial; there arrive caravans from Damascus, Aleppo and Egypt, especially during the silk-harvest season. A huge quantity is bought for their manufactories of satin and velvet and other cloth, of which there is a great consumption in the country, due to the magnificent clothes worn by the Turks. Without the epaulettes and embroidery of our wardrobes, their clothes are most beautiful, and very becoming to the wearers.

English Bombs and French Roads, 1858
Murray's Handbook

[Until] the beginning of the 17th centy. Beyrout scarcely ranked higher than a village; but the celebrated Druze prince Fakhr ed-Din, already so often mentioned in connexion with the towns on the coast, rebuilt it, made it the chief seat of his government, and erected a large palace, a fragment of which still stands near the eastern gate. This prince is also the traditional planter of the great pine-grove on the S. side of the city. He may probably have planted some trees there; but we have the historical evidence of the Arab author Edrisi that a forest of pines existed here as early as the 12th centy. There are only a few of the old trees remaining; but a large number of young ones are springing up, planted by direction of the Turkish authorities, who have somehow awakened to the necessity of checking the advances of the drifting sands.

The last episode in the history of Beyrout was its bombardment by the English fleet in September, 1840. The old walls were riddled with shot, and still remain so; several houses were destroyed; and the main object, the driving out of the troops of Ibrahim Pasha, was soon accomplished. The town speedily recovered from this disaster, and has since far outstripped in commercial enterprise and activity all the other cities of Syria. It is questionable whether at any time in its long history it was as prosperous as it is now. It is true its prosperity has not yet taken an architectural or an engineering turn. Its port remains blocked up with rubbish and stones, just as the fears of Fakhr ed-Din left it; there is not a street in the town, nor a road around it, fit for the employment of wheeled vehicles, by the use of which thousands of pounds might be saved annually; and the caravan *track*— it does not deserve the name of road—to the great city of Damascus is still among the very worst in Syria. There is some talk now about a French company which has undertaken to construct a carriage-road to Damascus. I have little faith in French companies, though this may succeed.

Physical Setting

Beirut has one thing in common with Manhattan: it is hard for the traveler arriving by ship to forget that first glimpse. In Beirut's case it is a gleaming white city on a tongue of land jutting out from the otherwise smooth coastline, with a dark-green backdrop of pine-covered mountains whose maternal arms enfold the city and its inhabitants. Today there may be more concrete than pines on the hills overlooking the city, but it remains a stunning sight.

Arrival in Beirut, 1737
Richard Pococke

The future Bishop Pococke left a rare and detailed account of the state of the city and its ruins before the nineteenth-century Ottoman infrastructure improvements (and a French road) obliterated many of the then surviving vestiges of the antique and medieval city.

We passed through a large grove of olive trees, and as we approached near Bayreut, I found the country exceedingly pleasant, being a rich soil, finely improved. About two miles before we came to this city, we passed through a fine grove of tall pines on the promontory; which, it is said, the famous Feckerdine [Fakhr al-Din] planted with his own hands, though it seems to be a mistake, as this grove is mentioned [by William of Tyre] as having been of great use to the Christians in besieging Bayreut, in the time of the holy war. A finer situation cannot be imagined; it is a green sod, and ends on the east side with a hanging ground over a beautiful valley, through which the river of Bayreut runs: the north end commands a view of the sea, and a prospect of the fine gardens of Bayreut to the northwest.

It is situated over the sea on a gentle rising ground, on the north side of a broad promontory. The gardens appear very beautiful on the hanging ground over it: The old port is a little bay, and was well secured by strong piers, which were destroyed by Feckerdine, as mentioned before; for he had possession of this city; and his successors, the princes of the Druses, have most of them been made governors of it, till of late years the Turks have thought it proper to take it out of their hands. To the east of the port is a castle built on two rocks in the sea, with a bridge to it. East of this, over the sea cliffs, is another castle; and to the east of that, are remains of a very large one, defended with a fossée [moat], where I saw some broken pillars. About a furlong to the east of this place, I came to the old city walls on that side. The town may be near two miles in circumference, and is defended with a very indifferent wall, which, on the west side, is built of hewn stone, with some small square towers, and part of it may be the remains of the ancient wall. At a little distance to the west of the town is a small bay, which opens to the north, where I saw some signs of ruins, but I could not judge what they were; it is possible the theatre built by Agrippa, might be here, and be contrived so as to have the advantage of the hill, like those of Pola and Frejus, and the sea may have washed it away. . . .

I . . . went to the east along the side of the bay; after having travelled about a league, we came to the place where, they say, Saint George killed the dragon which was about to devour the king of Bayreut's daughter. There is a mosque on the spot, which was formerly a Greek church; near it is a well, and they say, that the dragon usually came out of the hole, which is now the mouth of it. . . . In this mosque I saw an extraordinary ceremony performed on one of the Turks that was with me; who sitting down on the ground, the religious person, who had care of the mosque, took a piece of a small marble pillar, in which, they say, there is an extraordinary vertue against all sorts of pains, and rolled it on the back of the Turk for a considerable time.

A Comforting Flag, 1832
Alphonse de Lamartine

The poet Lamartine left a vivid account of his impressions during an extended stay in Beirut and elsewhere in the Levant; sadly, his daughter Julia died during the visit.

September 6 [1832]: nine o'clock in the morning. —We were before Beirout, one of the best-peopled towns on the coast of Syria, the ancient Berytus, made a Roman colony under Augustus, who gave it the name of Felix Julia. The epithet of "Fortunate" was bestowed upon it on account of the fertility of its surrounding lands, of its incomparable climate, and of the magnificence of its situation. The town occupies a delightful hill which sweeps with a gentle declivity to the sea; some banks of earth or of rocks advance into the waves, and support the Turkish fortifications, with an effect truly picturesque; the road is shut in by a tongue of land which defends it from the eastern winds. The whole of this tongue of land, as well as the neighbouring hills, are covered with the richest vegetation; mulberry-trees for silkworms are planted all around, raised in rows one above the other, upon artificial terraces; carob-trees, with their dark verdure and majestic dome; fig-trees, palms, oranges, pomegranates, and a quantity of other trees and shrubs foreign to our climates, extend on all parts of the shore near the sea the harmonious tints of their foliage.

At a greater distance, upon the acclivities of the mountains, forests of olives strew the country with their gray and ashy leaves. At about a league from the town, the high mountains of the chain of Lebanon begin to rise; they open their deep gorges where the eye loses itself in the distant darkness; they cast down their broad torrents, which become rivers; they stretch in different directions, some towards Tyre and Sidon, others towards Tripoli and Latakia, and their unequal summits, lost in the clouds, or whitened by the refraction of the sun's rays, resemble our Alps covered with eternal snows. . . .

The houses of the town arose in confused groups, the roofs of the lower serving as terraces for the upper ones. These houses with flat roofs, and some of them with turretted balustrades, the bars of painted wood which closed the windows hermetically with the veil of Eastern jealousy, the tops of palm-trees, which appeared to spring from the stones, and showed themselves even under the roofs, as if to carry a little verdure to the eyes of the females, prisoners in the harems—all this captivated us, and announced the East. We heard the sharp cry of the Arabs of the Desert who were disputing upon the quay, and the harsh and doleful groans of the camels, as they made them bend their knees to receive their loads. Occupied with this spectacle, so new and captivating to our eyes, we did not think of disembarking into our new country. The flag of France, however, floated on the top of a mast on one of the most elevated houses in the town, and appeared to invite us to go and repose ourselves after our long and painful voyage under its protection.

A Difficult Landing, 1838
Edouard Blondel

Arrival. At last Beirut came into view, with its crenelated walls flanked by towers, the minarets of its mosques looking almost Chinese. The city, on the gentle slope of a hill, extends down to the sea, where ruined castles give it the most picturesque aspect. One of them, built out from the town, is linked to the land by a dilapidated old bridge. The landscape is a graceful series of hills like terraces, covered with greenery and country houses, leading up towards the bald reddish-grey summits of Mount Lebanon. One's eye is surprised to discover convents and villages perched like eagles'-nests on rocky outcrops that one would have thought were inaccessible. All the way up to the highest peaks, you can see buildings standing out white against the azure sky: it is the most cheerful landscape imaginable, one more tranquil than any I had ever seen. . . .

The signal requesting a pilot was hauled up the mast, along with a cannon-shot to alert the populace; but nothing happened for a long time. After a long time, we made out a black dot visible when cresting the waves, rowed by three men; the sea was so wild that it took a long time before we could hear their shouts. Then came another difficulty: those people spoke neither English nor French, all they spoke was the local language, Arabic. . . .

The decrepit quay of Beirut, onto which we had more or less washed up, was the most animated place you could imagine, entirely full of people. All the inhabitants of the town seemed to have come along, their variegated, bizarre, and brightly-colored dress presenting a curious and unfamiliar spectacle to my eyes. They all seemed to follow our every movement with great interest; we understood it was because they had had no news from Europe or Egypt for several weeks. Those who know with what anxiety the daily post is awaited in the small towns of Europe, can only imagine the excitement produced by the monthly arrival of a packet-boat with dispatches.

Difficult Commuting, 1858
Murray's Handbook

The narrow lanes that wind through the gardens from villa to villa seem to have been made after the manner of the streets, as inconvenient as ingenuity could devise. They form a perfect labyrinth, which the stranger tries in vain to thread. In summer they are filled knee-deep with sand, and shut in by tall savage hedges of prickly-pear, excluding every breath of wind; so that in passing through them one feels as if walking amid the ashes of a half-extinct furnace. In winter every lane becomes a torrent-bed, sometimes impassable for man, and even dangerous for beast. Yet through them the Beyrout merchants plod along day after day, from their trim villas to their counting-houses in the city—each temporarily equipped as if for an aquatic excursion. It is amusing to mark the merchant's progress, here taking a flying-leap over a gulf; there making a desperate plunge; while yonder, where a kind of ferry has been established over a little lake, with half-a-dozen porters on each side as ferrymen, he is suddenly seized by 3 or 4, who keep up a running fight during the passage for their prey, the unfortunate passenger the while grasping energetically the neck and brawny shoulders of some one of them, and trying to keep the others off with the stiff point of his umbrella. Still Beyrout is a thriving town; and it may in time possess the luxury of streets and roads. Until it gets these it is, of course, folly to talk of introducing wheeled vehicles.

What to Expect, 1876
Baedeker 1876

Arrival. The entrance to the bay of Beirut is magnificent. In the background towers the majestic Lebanon, with the snow-clad Sannin. The hotels send their agents on board, and to them luggage had better be entrusted for clearance at the custom-house. The landing is conducted in a more orderly way than at Yafa. From the douane [customs-house] the traveller turns to the right and ascends the street of the Christians.

Hotels. Hotel d'Orient, kept by Nicolas Bassul, an obliging Arab, who speaks a few words of many different languages; Hotel Bellevue, the property of Andrea Bucopulos, a Greek. Both these houses are beautifully situated on the coast, at the S. end of the town. The accommodation and wines are good at both. Charge 15 fr. per day. Of the second class, frequented by Levantine merchants: Hotel de l'Europe or Derricadere, also a restaurant, kept by a Frenchman, in the house of Bustros.

Beer and Coffee Houses, chiefly situated on the coast near the hotels, and kept by Greeks, not recommended.

Their visitors are frequently enlivened by Bohemian bands of music. Prots, the restaurateur of the German club, keeps the best cafe in the place.

Of the Arabian Cafes one on the Ras Beirut near the Prussian hospital and those near the douane may be mentioned, owing to their fine situation. Cup of coffee 20–30 paras; nargileh the same. Those near the douane afford the best opportunity for observing the habits of the native population. . . .

Beirut (or Berut) is the most important seaport and commercial town in Syria, and the large bay looking towards the N. affords the best anchorage on the Syrian coast. The town, beautifully situated on a slight eminence , occupies a considerable part of the S. side of this bay. Beyond the narrow plain of the coast the mountains rise rapidly, and beyond them rises the broad, snow-clad Jebel Sannin. They are furrowed by several deep ravines, but are cultivated to a considerable height. The rosy tint of the mountains contrasting with the deep blue of the sea presents a most picturesque scene by evening light.

While the scenery resembles that of Italy, the climate of Beirut is genial and seldom oppressively hot. Much rain falls in winter, but the crocus, cyclamen, and other flowers thrive at that season, and palms are frequently seen in the neighbouring gardens. . . . The heat is always tempered by a fresh sea breeze; and, as the nights are mild, sleeping with open windows is not attended with the same risk as in many other places. Many of the Europeans settled at Beirut remove to 'Aleih, Bhamdun, or other heights of Lebanon for the summer months, where they sometimes camp in tents.

Arriving by Land, 1878
Gabriel Charmes

Of all the cities in Syria, the one that has been most often described is Beirut. Travellers arriving directly from Europe usually disembark at its port; and one could hardly think of a better way to begin a voyage.

If one arrives by land from Sidon, as we did, one is deprived of the vivid impression that strikes one at first sight of the admirable gulf of Beirut, one of the most beautiful in the Mediterranean. The road is charming for all that. . . . Leaving Sidon, we travelled so close to the sea that the horses had to walk in the water, to avoid the quicksand of the beach one has to travel on, there being no other path. The fragrance of orange-blossom followed us in our morning jaunt through the famous orchards of Sidon. . . . No sooner had we crossed the Damour River than we found ourselves in a country of mulberry-trees. The plain is covered with them, and as we proceeded we found ourselves lost amid green freshness. From time to time we could glimpse, through the branches, the little huts where the silkworms work their magic. A pictur-esque Arab came out to watch us pass; a lovely girl in a shining costume hid behind a tree; a ray of sunlight shone through to enliven the surrounding shade. Then we found ourselves back on the beach.

In the distance, a long reddish cliff appeared, catch-ing the light, looming over the sea: Beirut! But we're not there yet. We paused a while at Nabi Yunus, where Jonas is supposed to have been spat out by the whale. . . . Our own hunger hurried us on to the next stop, at Khan el-Khaldeh, a moderately comfortable caravansaray where we could cook a little food under the arches of a decrepit building, listening to the sea beating at our feet and watching the sun set fire to the silhouette of Beirut. From there the landscape gets steadily more beautiful, and more representative of our preconceived notion of the East than any other. The colors are more vivid even than the dreams we have while sitting in our European mists. The landscape, the sands we walk through, then the plain, beyond it the mountain backdrop to our journey with its startlingly almost blood-red hue making the colors around us more vivid. . . . The blue of the sea, the green of the forest, the thousand shades of the gardens, all retained their original intensity; we felt as though we had entered a new country. . . .

Life seems to overflow from the picturesque hills, covered with houses and gardens—it could have been a corner of Phoenicia, in antiquity. As we came to the first streets of Beirut, we had no doubt we were in modern Syria: a modern city, produced by Eastern taste, translated into bizarre buildings, a constant mixture of

parvenu elegance and naïve poverty, European fantasies
and memories of Asia, unexpected mingling of all genres,
all styles, all fashions—and despite all the clashes, an
inescapable charm, an irresistible attraction!

A Magnificent Setting, 1858
Murray's Handbook

The situation of Beyrout is exceedingly beautiful, especially as viewed from the sea. The promontory on which
it stands is triangular, the apex projecting some 3 m. into
the Mediterranean, and the base running along the foot
of Lebanon. The south-western side, which is wholly
composed of loose drifting sand, and has all the aspect
of a desert. The north-western side is totally different,
the shore-line is formed of a range of irregular, deeply-
indented rocks and cliffs, worn into a thousand fantastic
forms by the waves—here, deep gloomy caverns into
which the waters roll with a roar as of distant thunder;
there, jagged isolated rocks, and bold precipices, around
which the white surf plays like a thing of life, sending up
showers of spray that sparkle like diamonds in the bright

sunlight. Behind these rocks the ground rises gradually for a mile or more, when it attains the height of about 200 ft. In the middle of the shore-line stands the city—first a dense nucleus of buildings surrounded by an old tottering wall; then a broad *nebula* of picturesque villas, embowered in rich foliage, running up to the very summit of the heights, and extending far to the rt. and l. Beyond these are the mulberry groves covering the whole acclivities; and variegated here and there by a few graceful palms and dark cypresses.

The old town stands on the very beach, and often during a northerly gale gets more of the sea water than is agreeable. The little port, now in a great measure filled up, lies between a projecting cliff and a ruinous insulated tower called Burj Fanzar, which bears, like the rest of the fortifications, many a mark of British bullets. The walls of the town were never strong, and are of no use at the present day except as impediments to commerce, for which beneficent object the Turks seem inclined to keep them up. The streets are narrow, gloomy, dirty, and badly paved; and so steep and tortuous withal, that almost every bale and package landed at the custom-house has to be carried off on the backs of men! The houses are substantially built of stone; and a few of the villas in the suburbs possess some little pretensions to architectural effect; though it must be admitted the Beyrouthines do not excel in this branch of the arts. The view commanded by the higher houses is truly magnificent, embracing the bay of St Georges; the indented coast, retiring, promontory on promontory, till lost in the distance; and the noble ridge of Lebanon, with its wild glens, and dark pine-forests, and clustering villages, and castle-like convents, and snow-capped peaks on which the clouds sleep.

Lift Up Thine Eyes, 1878
Gabriel Charmes

Despite all the transformations which Beirut has undergone and will do in the future, the city will never lose the charm of its surrounding nature. . . . Just sit on the terrace of a hotel or of someone's well-situated house, or just look out from your window or balcony, and you will see the reddish curve of the gulf contrasting with the blue of the sea; then a little further up, the green gardens dotted with points of light; then beyond it all, rising gently, the diverse levels of the mountain with its harmonious blend of colors, until finally your eyes rise up to the white summits of Sannin, covered in sparkling snow, rising up above it all like a giant tent in the middle of an encampment.

Picturesque Scene, 1894
Baedeker 1894

Beirut occupies a considerable part of the S. side of St. George's Bay, which looks towards the N. The interior of the bay offers a certain protection against bad weather to the ships which have to anchor in the open roads. In the summer of 1889, a French company began the construction of a good harbour.

Beirut is the most important commercial town of Syria. In 1888 there ran into the port: 2767 sailing vessels of 45,846 tons, and 494 steam vessels of 501,368 tons. It is believed that this number will be considerably increased on the completion of the new harbour, which will be the only safe landing-place between Port Sa'id and Alexandretta.

— The chief importance of Beirut lies in its imports. The only articles exported in large quantities are grain, silk (1888: 2600 bales), and wool (1888: 3500 bales).

Beirut is the chief town of the Wilayet [governorate] of the same name, the residence of the Wali [governor], and has a garrison of 400 infantry and 80 cavalry. —The town is the seat of a Greek Orthodox bishop, a Maronite archbishop, a United Greek patriarch, and a Papal Delegate (Msgr. Piavi, who is also patriarch of Jerusalem).

The town is beautifully situated on the slopes of Ras Beirut and St. Dimitri, facing the sea. The plain is covered with luxuriant gardens. Beyond them the mountains rise rapidly, overtopped by the snow-clad summits of the Sannin and Keneiseh. The hills are furrowed by several deep ravines, but are cultivated to a considerable height. The rosy tint of the mountains contrasting with the deep blue of the sea presents a most picturesque scene by evening light.

The Grand Tour

From the late eighteenth century, the Great and the Good of European society often added a Levantine chapter to their tour of notable places; all of them seem to have felt a compulsion to share their impressions and experiences in writing, and many devoted considerable energy to criticism of those left by previous travelers.

Beirut Condemned to Be Miserable, 1784
C. F. Volney

The first thing you see as you travel along the coast from Tripoli, is the city of Beryte, which the Arabs pronounce as the ancient Greeks did: "Bairout". It is situated on a plain which sticks out from the foot of Mount Lebanon like a point into the sea, about two leagues out from the general line of the coast. . . .

The dialect of the inhabitants is justly renowned as the worst one of all: in itself one finds every one of the twelve defects of elocution identified by the Arab grammarians.

The port of Beirut, like all those along the coast made up by a jetty, is like the others filled up with sand and ruins. The town is encircled by a wall of such soft sandstone that it gives way before a cannon-ball without collapsing, to the great disappointment of the Russians when they attacked. These old walls leave the city defenceless, in fact. There are two other disadvantages which condemn Beirut to be forever a miserable place: it is surrounded by a chain of hills running down towards the south-east; and the fact that it lacks sources of water. Women have to trudge a quarter of an hour outside the city to find water, at a spring which is none too good. . . .

One finds—outside the walls to the west—ruins and some column-barrels, all proving that Beirut was once much larger than it is today. The plain which makes up its hinterland is entirely planted with white mulberry-trees, which (unlike those of Tripoli) are young and vigorous, given that under the Druze administration they used to be replanted regularly. That ensures that the silk they produce is of an excellent quality. . . . In summer, staying in Beirut is very uncomfortable as a result of the heat and the tepid water. Nonetheless it is not unhealthy, though they say it once was; however, the Emir Fakhr al-Din planted a forest of pine-trees which still survives a league from the city.

A Queenly Tailor's Wife, 1851
Gérard de Nerval

When we had come out of quarantine, I rented an apartment for three months in the house of some Maronite

Christians about half a league from the town. Most of these houses, situated amid gardens, standing in rows along terraces planted with mulberry-trees, look like little manor-houses of the feudal period, solidly built of brownish stone with loopholes and arches. Outside staircases lead to the different floors, each of which has a terrace of its own, until you reach that which is at the top of the whole house, where the families gather in the evening to enjoy the view over the gulf.

On every side was thick glossy verdure, with only the regular hedges of nopals [prickly pears] to mark the divisions. The first days we were there I gave myself up completely to the enjoyment of the coolness and shade. Everywhere around us there seemed to be life and comfort; the women well dressed, beautiful and unveiled, going and coming with those heavy pitchers which they fill at the cisterns, and carry gracefully upon their shoulders. Our hostess, who wore upon her head a kind of cone draped with a shawl, which, with the tresses of long hair adorned with sequins, gave her the air of an Assyrian queen, was only the wife of a tailor who kept a shop in Beyrouth.

Religion and Holy Places

In the Levant, one was, and to a large extent still is, defined by one's religious affiliation more than by one's nationality: "I am a Sunni from Damascus" or "a Druze from the Hauran" or "an Orthodox from Latakieh." This policy enabled the Ottomans to govern a huge area with very few 'boots on the ground,' as most civil matters were left to each sect's ecclesiastical authorities. During the long period of Ottoman decline, this provided the European powers with a golden opportunity to meddle, each choosing a sympathetic minority to champion: the French

the Maronites, the British the Druzes, etc. The legacy of this is still visible today, and was very much in evidence when our travelers passed through.

European Assimilation, 1878
Gabriel Charmes

Despite its modern disguise, Beirut has remained a city of the Middle Ages. Each neighborhood is dominated by its convent or church, less elegant than in the past but they compensate for this in size. I know of no other city, except Jerusalem, which is so drenched in religious atmosphere. But Jerusalem still retains its antique flavor; it's a kind of ruined relic of the past. In Beirut, religion permeates every action of modern life. It doesn't only dominate the present, it fashions the future. All the schools are of one sect or another, and so are the politics. One belongs to a certain party because one belongs to the corresponding religion or sect. No-one is Syrian: the Muslims are assimilated to the Turks; the Christians are French, Austrians, Italians or Russians; the Druzes are English; the Amaris and Metualis [Shia Muslims], not being protected by any Great Power, don't know what their nationality is, to their infinite chagrin.

Even children among themselves speak of being French, English, Russian, or Turkish, depending on whether they are Catholic, Druze or Muslim. Those members of fringe groups or sects which have no such protection are treated like pariahs, or stateless persons. Thus the Greek Catholics, for example, who are few in number, are overwhelmed by the invasive personality of the Maronites, and are sometimes treated with disdain by more fortunate communities.

A Beard Story, 1697
Henry Maundrell

From this tower we had a view of the whole city: amongst other prospects it yielded us the sight of a large Christian church, said to have been at first consecrated to St. John the Evangelist. But, it being now usurp'd by the Turks for their chief mosque, we could not be permitted to see it, otherwise than at this distance. Another church there is in the town, which seems to be ancient; but being a very mean fabrick is suffer'd to remain still in the hands of the Greeks. . . . We found it adorn'd with abundance of old pictures. But that which appear'd most observable was a very odd figure of a saint, drawn at full length, with a large beard reaching down to his feet. The curate gave us to understand that this was St. Nicephorus; and perceiving that his beard was the chief object of our admiration, he gratified us with the following relation concerning him, viz. that he was a person of the most eminent virtues in his time. But his great misfortune was, that the endowments of his mind were not set off with the outward ornament of a beard. Upon occasion of which defect, he fell into a deep melancholy. The devil taking the advantage of this priest, promised to give him that boon which nature had deny'd, in case he would comply with his suggestions. The beardless saint, tho' he was very desirous of the reward propos'd, yet he would not purchase it at that rate neither: but rejected the previous bribe with indignation, declaring resolutely, that he had rather for ever despair of his wish than obtain it upon such terms. And at the same time, taking in his hand the downy tuft upon his chin, to witness the stability of his resolution (for he had it seems beard enough to swear by) behold! as a reward for his constancy, he found the hair immediately stretch, with the pluck that he gave it. Whereupon finding it in so good a humour, he follow'd the happy omen: and as young heirs that have been niggardly bred, generally turn prodigals when they come to their estates; so he never desisted from pulling his beard, till he had wiredrawn it down to his feet.

Uncomfortable Bedfellows, 1894
Baedeker 1894

Before the slaughter of the Christians in 1860, Beirut had about 20,000 inhabitants, the number now exceeds 100,000. The official statistics for 1889 give : Muslims 33,000; Greek Orthodox 30,000; Maronites 28,000; Melkites (United Greeks) 9,000; Jews 1500; Latins 1500; Protestants 900; Syrian-Catholics 600; Armenian Catholics 400; Druses 300; other religious communities 300, total 105,400; 6 hospitals, 23 mosques, 36 Christian churches, 66 boys' and 36 girls' schools with 8000 boys and 6175 girls, of these 21 boys' and 2 girls' schools are Muslim institutions with 2000 boys and 500 girls. — There are about 2000 Europeans in Beirut.

The Muslim element is gradually being displaced by the Christian. The Christians of Beirut are very industrious, apparently possessing a share of the commercial enterprise of the ancient Phoenicians. Many of the firms have branches in England, Marseilles, and elsewhere, and compete successfully with the European merchants settled in Syria. Italian was formerly the commonest language here, next to Arabic, but it is now being displaced by French, as many of the Roman Catholic Christians have their children educated in the Lazarist and other good French schools. The percentage of persons who cannot read or write is comparatively low at Beirut, and the highly important work of educating the female sex has been efficiently begun.

As evidence of the intellectual activity of the people it may be added that 13 printing offices (the best are the Jesuit and the American) exist in Beirut, and 12 Arabic newspapers find readers.

Promenades and Excursions

Visitors have always broken their stay in the crowded port city with excursions: at the city's edge, they all visited the Pine Forest: there is still a copse of parasol pines, called Hirsh al-Snawbar, along the coast and inward to the south of the city center. It is a bedraggled remnant of a great forest that legend (and many travelers) attribute to the

seventeenth-century Druze emir Fakhr al-Din, but which was there in antiquity. Or they rode out to close attractions like the Nahr al-Kalb ('Dog River') and its fascinating series of carvings left by various conquerors from Ramesses II to Bonaparte; some made longer jaunts over the mountains to Baalbek, wonder of the ancient world.

Landscape of Dreams, 1832
Alphonse de Lamartine

About half a league from the town on the east, the Emir Fakardin had planted a forest of spreading pines, upon a sandy ridge which extends between the sea and the plain of Bagdad, a pretty Arab village at the foot of Lebanon. The emir had planted this magnificent forest, it is said, in order to oppose a rampart to the invasion of the immense hillocks of red sand which rise at a little distance, and threaten to overwhelm Beirout and its rich plantations. The forest has become superb: the trunks of the trees are sixty and eighty feet high, and their wide immovable branches stretch from one to another, covering an immense space with their shade; the sand creeps between the trunks, and forms the pleasantest soil for the hoofs of the horses. The rest of the ground is covered with a light downy turf, sprinkled with flowers of the most dazzling red; the roots of wild hyacinth are so large, that they are not crushed beneath the iron of the horses' shoes. Through the columns of trunks we see on one side the white and reddish downs of sand which hide the sea, on the other the plain of Bagdad, and the course of the river into this plain, and a corner of the gulf, looking like a small lake, so much is it lessened by the horizon of land, and the twelve or fifteen Arab villages upon the last slopes of Lebanon, which form the curtain of this scene.

The light is so clear, and the air so pure, that we distinguish at several leagues' elevation the forms of the trees upon the mountains, and the eagles who float on the ethereal ocean without moving their wings. This wood of pines is certainly the most magnificent of all the spots I have seen in my life. The sky, the mountains, the snows, the blue horizon of the sea, the red and lurid aspect of the desert; the meandering course of the river, the isolated tops of the cypress-trees, the clusters of palms in the fields, the delightful appearance of the huts, covered with oranges and vines overhanging the roofs; the austere aspect of the elevated Maronite monasteries, casting alternate shade and light on the chiselled rocks of Lebanon; the caravans of camels loaded with merchandise passing in silence amongst the trees; flocks of poor Jews mounted on asses, holding two children on each arm; women enveloped in white veils on horseback, marching to the sound of the fife and the tambour, surrounded by a crowd of children, dressed in red stuffs embroidered with gold, and dancing before their horses; some Arab horsemen throwing the *djerid* around us, upon horses whose manes literally sweep the sand; some groups of Turks seated before a cafe built in the foliage, and smoking their pipes, or performing their devotions; a little farther, the sandy desert hills without end, which are tinged with the golden rays of the evening sun, and from which the wind raises clouds of heated dust; and, *in fine*, the dull murmur of the sea, which mingles with the musical rustling of the wind amongst the branches of the pines, and with the song of myriads of unknown birds—all this offers to the eye and the thought of the wanderer a blending of objects the most sublime and beautiful, and at the same time the most melancholy, which have ever excited my mind: it is the site of my dreams; I will return to it every day.

Favorite Excursion, 1876
Baedeker 1876

The favourite walk and drive at Beirut is the road of the French Company as far as the Pines, where there are numerous cafes. The most frequented is by the second group of pines, where a Lebanese band plays every Friday in winter. This "Pineta", or grove of pines (*pinus halebensis*) bounds the S. side of the town, affording a protection against the encroachment of the sand from the S., and is said to have been planted for that purpose by the Druse prince Fakhr ed-Din. The French troops were encamped here in 1861.

A beautiful walk of 1 hr. may also be taken to the hill which extends across the plain from the sea near the quarantine to the pines. . . . The hill is cultivated and overgrown with trees and shrubs. It commands a delightful view of the bay of Beirut and the extensive town stretching towards the promontory. In the opposite direction rises Mt. Lebanon. The most northern part of the hill, where a more open space is reached (5 min.) near a cemetery and some pines, affords the finest view. We may return thence to Beirut by the road leading to the river.

We're Not in Egypt Any More, 1849
Gustave Flaubert

Beirut. The houses are made of stone: we're not in Egypt any more. I don't know what makes me think of the Crusades. Hotel Battista, in the Port. To the right, a fort on the sea, demolished by the English. There's a battle for watermelons newly arrived from Jaffa. The children who spend all day swimming sport turbans made from floating watermelon rinds. At the hotel, the Austrian counsellor, . . . a Russian, a Maltese captain, the Italian emigrant who impresses me as a ruffian and quite happily pockets our 50 francs.

The bazaars: bumping, crowding, very raffish; silk everywhere. Ramadan nights: mechanical toys in the café, the noise they make. We drink melted snow.

At the cemetery, one evening, as the sun set, three sheep grazing on the grass among the tombstones. An Arab reclining on a tomb with two or three others playing jokes around him, smoking and drinking their coffee quite blissfully. A road that goes between and even over the graves; the sea, greenery and Beirut on the right, bushes everywhere. A thin old man with a grey beard, clicking his rosary on a tombstone. An enclosure with two graves, a tent covering to protect them.

Picnic on the grass at the Pine Forest. Watching monks pass by with their heads covered with kerchiefs, then camels: violet sky over the mountains, through the trees.

Bride of the Sea, 1858
J. Lewis Farley

The favourite, indeed the only walk here, is to the west of the town, along the sea-shore, on the Ras-el-Beyrout. Here, at the various cafés, you can, as you pass, contemplate the picturesque costumes of the people, and observe the ease and grace of their various attitudes, as they sip their coffee and inhale the aroma of the fragrant tobacco of Jebeil [Byblos]. Some remain within doors, others recline upon the grass, or seat themselves on the rocks overhanging the sea, forming everywhere groupings the most various and picturesque.

A little way beyond the French consulate, passing the Mohammedan burial-ground on the right, is the dockyard, where a great number of men are constantly employed in ship-building. This branch of industry increases visibly, as from Beirut the entire coasting trade is supplied with ships. A curious superstition is connected with this. The Arab sailors look upon the ship as "the bride of the sea," into whose arms she must pass pure and unstained, or woe to the unfortunate mariners! If, however, a frail damsel were permitted to place her foot on board the virgin bark, and repeat certain words, all her own sins would be at once transferred to the future bride, the erring damsel herself becoming pure again. In order to prevent this, when the ship is completed and ready for launching, she is watched closely night and day, until she is consigned, pure and spotless, to her powerful bridegroom.

Ride to the Nahr el-Kelb, 1858
Murray's Handbook

A tolerable "back," and a guide of sufficient intelligence for a day's excursion, are easily procured at any of the Beyrout hotels—mounting the one, and following the other, we scamper off to the romantic glen of the "Dog River." About a mile from the town we are shown the remains of an old brick building, which has, somehow or other, been linked to the legend of *St. George and the Dragon*, in which every loyal Englishman will feel a home interest. Some affirm the Dragon was slain on this spot; but others affirm that the combat took place on the neighbouring beach, and the victorious saint came here to wash his hands. The guide will probably relate both versions, with perhaps a few extempore variations of his own; appending the all but universal Arab axiom, *Ullah by'arif* [God knows]. . . .

Inscriptions and Sculptures at Nahr el-Kelb. The rocky ridge on the S. bank of Nahr el-Kelb projects considerably into the sea, terminating in a cliff about 100 ft. high. On approaching it from Beyrout, we observe to the rt. and l. numerous excavations in the rock, like quarries. The old road, which still forms the only means of passage, winds up the steep slope, runs along the very edge of the cliff, and descends a yet steeper bank on the N. side. It is everywhere hewn in the rock; in some places there is a deep cutting, and in others the surface is merely leveled. It is 6 ft. wide, and is paved with large stones, that may have been smooth at one time; but now they seem as if placed there only to break the legs of unfortunate animals. On the summit of the pass, overhanging the sea, is a rude pedestal, and beside it a prostrate column with an illegible Latin inscription—apparently a Roman milestone. Popular tradition however, trying to account for the name of the river, informs us that the image of a "Dog" once stood here; and the guide will point it out, its black head just appearing above the waves, far below. Most people will have difficulty in recognizing any trace of likeness to a dog, or other beast, in that "rock of the ocean." . . .

Some tell us that in long-past ages a monster of the wolf species was chained by some god or demon at the river's mouth, which, when lashed to fury by the storms, awoke the echoes of far-distant Cyprus with his bark. Others say that the sharp shocks of the waves on the cavernous cliffs gave rise to both the name and the legend. And another story is that the statue of a dog formerly stood on the pedestal that crowns the cliff; its mouth being wide open, strange sounds were wont to issue from it when the winds were high; these the Arabs long regarded as supernatural warnings of impending woe; but at length, on one occasion, they mustered courage, assembled in a body, and hurled the monster into the sea. . . .

Descending on the N. side, we soon see some remarkable tablets to the rt., which we leave for the present, and pass on towards the modern bridge. Before reaching it a beautifully cut Latin inscription attracts our attention on the base of a low cliff to the right of the path. It is still perfect, with the exception of a portion of a single line purposefully erased; and we learn from it the important fact that this road was made in the reign of the Emperor Marcus Aurelius Antoninus, who it appears, was a special benefactor of Syria. . . .

We now return to take a glance at still more interesting relics of antiquity—the *sculptured tablets*. A short examination shows us that the Emperor Aurelius was not the only royal road-maker who scaled the pass of the Nahr el-Kelb. The traces of a much more ancient road are seen higher up the cliff, quite distinct on the northern side of the promontory, but obliterated on the southern, probably from the falling of some of the rocks. It can now only be ascended on foot, and even

thus it is not very easy to scale it. The sculptured tablets are found at intervals on the smooth faces of the
rocks, on the upper side of the *old* road. They are *nine*
in number, of which 3 are regarded as Egyptian and 6 as
Assyrian. They are of different sizes and shapes, but all
large enough to contain life-size figures. Commencing at
the northern base of the pass, the first 3 tablets are close
to the present road, which so far runs in the line of the
more ancient one. The old road then strikes up to the l.
over steep, rugged rocks, and we must follow it to visit
the remaining sculptures.

A Baalbek Diversion, 1722
Jean de la Roque

*There is one excursion from Beirut that every Grand Tourist,
Pilgrim, or visitor of any stripe and era had to make before
moving on: Baalbek. Ancient Heliopolis of the Romans, it
was a center of high religious devotion (to the Olympian
Gods with an Eastern flavor), so monumental that the sheer
size of the ruins still astonishes today.*

We walked then for about three hours crossing the plain at a diagonal, and arrived in Baalbeck quite late and very tired on the last day of October.

We went first to the house of the Sheikh who had already retired in his rooms. . . . He received us kindly, quickly reading the letter we had given him, then after a speech of welcome, and after we presented him some rosaries made with handsome coco wood beads, he offered us coffee according to the tradition in the country. This closed the ceremony, as he retired soon after to leave us free to go take a much-needed rest.

On leaving that room we went into another where we saw a dinner set on a platform or sofa; a moment later we were served a soup made with rice and milk, and two other dishes of vegetables stewed in oil, with olives and cheese; at the end they brought huge pomegranates, and grapes of outstanding beauty and taste. I had never tasted better bread or drunk more pleasant or refreshing wine than at that meal. One of the Sheikh's officers kept us company then led us each to his room where we found beds that were quite good enough. . . .

[The next morning] he asked us the purpose of our trip, and what could he do to help. We thought it best not to evade the answer but rather to tell him simply what brought us to Baalbeck; which pleased much the Sheikh who liked inquisitive and intellectual people. He does not share the opinion of those other Moslems, who believe that the Franks come searching for treasures in the ruins of ancient buildings, and are also acting as spies to help the Christian princes in taking over their country in reporting on fortified areas. He nonetheless advised us not to talk to anyone about our curiosity, because many people might be offended by it. He promised to give us all possible assistance so that we could start our visits the next day. . . . We had dinner with him in a light, slightly elevated, entirely beautiful sitting room with a domed ceiling. In the middle of the hall, an ornamental marble fountain spouted water high up towards the dome. The furniture one saw was a large platform or sofa covered in Persian carpets, with large red velvet cushions framed in golden fringes; opposite stood another platform differently decorated, where we sat to eat on a carpet, in the oriental style.

The Sheikh offered us a sumptuous meal. Whereas most of the stews seemed quite different from ours, the sweets were excellent and best of all, after the meat and to end the meal we were served a number of Damascus jams and native fruits. I mustn't forget to mention the wine, which was one of the best in Lebanon and which the Sheikh gave us most straightforwardly, contrary to the use of the Moslems who do not like to share a meal with people drinking wine. He allowed us to drink to his health, and at the end of the meal toasted us with a small glass of rossoly [a distilled concoction of flower, sugar, and spices to which brandy was added], a gift from some English guests which he also wanted us to taste.

After the meal, coffee was served and the conversation was carried on quite pleasantly as the Sheikh made some witty and complimentary remarks on the French Nation which he called the queen of the western Nations, mentioning at all times the greatness and power of our "Emperor" as he insisted on calling him. . . . Finally they brought tobacco with pipes; the Sheikh said he knew that Frankish monks do not smoke, but gave me his pipe already burning (which is a special favour in the Levant), adding with a laugh: "This poor Maronite will keep me company." He had understood all along that I was a Frenchman disguised a Maronite. After smoking, we took our leave and went back to the Maronite church where the mass lasted a long time, keeping us late into the night.

Murder in the Temple, 1737
Richard Pococke

The famous temple of Baalbeck, which has been so often mentioned by travellers, is a most exquisite piece of workmanship, on which the utmost art has been bestowed. . . . It is built of a fine white stone, that approaches very near to the nature of marble, but grows yellow once exposed to the air. . . .

The several members of the columns and pedestals of the pilasters, both within and without, are carried all round the building, and the whole temple is built as on one solid basement. The ground is risen near to the top of the basement, both within and without, except on the south side without, where the basement is seen in all its proportions. . . . I went down into the vaults under this part by the light of candles; they consist of two rooms; going into the inner vault I was startled to see a dead body lie in its clothes; the murther was committed about six months before by a Greek for the sake of his money, and the body was never removed.

Poetic Inspiration in the Ruins, 1833
Alphonse de Lamartine

Lamartine's daughter Julia died in Beirut on 7 December 1832, leaving him to begin his journey to Baalbek and Damascus in a melancholy vein.

On the 28th March [1833] I left Beirout for Balbek and Damascus. The caravan was composed of twenty-six horses, and eight or ten Arabs on foot, as domestics and escort. On quitting Beirout, we proceeded by deep roads through a red sand, the margins of which were festooned with all the flowers of Asia in the beauty and fragrance of spring. . . . The same route as the last ride I had with Julia. . . .

On drawing near to Anti-Lebanon, the plain rises, and becomes more dry and rocky. Anemones and snow-drops were as plentiful as pebbles under our feet. We began to descry an immense mass, which stood out in black relief from the white sides of Anti-Lebanon. It was Balbek, but we could distinguish nothing yet. At last we reached the first ruin. It was a small octagon temple, supported on columns of red Egyptian granite, evidently cut from more lofty columns, some having arched capitals, and others no trace of the arch, and having been, in my opinion, transported, cut, and erected there in very modern times, to bear the cupola of a Turkish mosque, or the roof of a dervish's dwelling. . . . This temple is a quarter of an hour's march from Balbek. Impatient to behold what remotest antiquity has left us of the beautiful, the grand, and the mysterious, we pressed forward our wearied horses, whose hoofs began to clash against blocks of marble, trunks of columns, and prostrated capitals. All the walls enclosing the fields in the vicinity of Balbek are raised with these relics; our antiquaries would find each stone an enigma. . . .

We skirted one of the sides of this hill of ruins, on which a multitude of graceful columns arose, gilded by the setting sun, and recalling to the mind the yellow and dull hues of the marble of the Parthenon, or of the Coliseum at Rome. Amongst these columns there were some in long elegant rows, still bearing their capitals untouched, their cornices richly sculptured, and extending along the marble walls which encompassed the sanctuaries. Others were leaning entire against these walls, which sustained them, like a tree whose roots have been loosened, but whose stem is still healthy and strong. But the greatest number were scattered in immense heaps of marble or stone upon the slopes of the hill, in the deep ditches which surround it, and even in the bed of the river flowing at its foot. At the summit of the stony eminence six columns of a more gigantic size stand isolated, not far from the lower temple, and yet preserve their colossal cornices; we shall hereafter inquire to what these bear testimony, in their isolation from the other edifices.

On prolonging our stroll along the foot of the monuments, we found the columns and architectural remains conclude, and we saw nothing but prodigious walls, built of enormous stones, and almost all bearing traces of sculpture; the relics of another era, of which they made use at the remote epoch when they reared the temples which are not in ruins. . . .

We arose with the sun whose first rays fell upon the temple of Balbek, and imparted to those mysterious ruins that brilliancy of renewed youth which nature can render at its pleasure, even to what time has destroyed. After a hasty breakfast, we departed to touch with our hands what we had as yet only seen with our eyes. . . . We knew not where to rest our eyes. All around were marble doors of a prodigious height and breadth; windows or niches bordered with the most admirable sculpture; arches worked with exquisite ornaments; pieces of cornices, entablatures, and capitals, thick as dust beneath our feet; domes springing above our heads—all was mystery, confusion, and disorder; the masterpieces of art, the relics of ages, inexplicable wonders were around us!

We felt what we were in comparison with the mass and eternity of these monuments—like the swallows, which nestle a season in the interstices of these blocks of stone, ignorant for or by whom they have been there collected. The ideas which have reared these masses, and accumulated these heaps, are unknown to us; the dust of the marble that we tread upon knows more than we, but can tell us nothing; and in a few ages, the generations who shall come to visit in their turn the remains of our monuments of the present era, will likewise ask, without being able to answer, why we have built and sculptured. . . .

Balbek, March 29, midnight. I went yesterday to the hill of temples, by the light of the moon, to think, to weep, and to pray. . . . This stupendous overthrown monument of humanity, on the wrecks of which I was seated, inspired me with such strong and ardent sentiments, that they almost of themselves escaped in verse, the natural language of my thoughts when they master me.

Baalbek, 1838
Edouard Blondel

Monuments are no more fortunate than men in escaping the ravages of time. Baalbek, a temple originally dedicated to the Sun, where masses of people used to crowd in to witness the sacrifice; Baalbek, whose prestigious architecture added glory to the religious ceremonies within its precinct; Baalbek found itself transformed, mercilessly converted into a fortress. To do this all that was needed was to close a few passages between its thick walls, reaching as they do seventy to eighty feet tall. They hollowed out arrow-slits, chopped in crenellations, and then surrounded the whole thing with a moat. The First Roman Legion must have bivouacked there, for you can still read over a doorway: "*Centuria Prima.*" The religious silence that had previously held sway here was replaced by the tumult of war, the clash of arms, the shouts of combatants. Then earthquakes joined man in the desecration of this admirable edifice, and only once the destruction was complete, was it abandoned to the bats and jackals.

Today Baalbek is nothing but a maze of shattered columns, of fallen capitals and every sort of colossal debris. How could I express the fine workmanship of each fragment lying mutilated in the dust, over which we tread willy-nilly? The least among them deserve to be excavated with respect, to enrich the museums and antique cabinets of Europe.

Nothing of the great temple still stands except for the six columns which one discovers on arriving to Baalbek. They are seventy-two feet high, and more than twenty-four feet around. The three drums of white granite they are carved from have been so tightly fused together by iron rods, that you cannot pry a knife-blade between them. Capitals of the most ornate Corinthian order still support the superstructure, on which one can see the heads of lions, giant gargoyles with gaping mouths. The walls of this edifice, made of enormous yellowish limestone blocks, contain a myriad of niches; the scalloped vaulting can hardly cover the debris of statues hacked to pieces and totally destroyed. There are everywhere friezes and cornices of various patterns, all extremely graceful.

Next to the great temple, there is a smaller one, with its enclosure and most of its columns still intact. Its shape is rectangular; its walls, about sixty feet high, have (with one exception) neither doors nor windows. Around the whole there is a portico with twelve granite columns on each long side, with six on the others. . . . There is nothing in either Italy or Greece to compete with the architectural riches of Baalbek. Only a sudden rain-shower such as the one that burst upon us could have induced us to leave these ruins, where we otherwise would have wandered many more hours; it is all so full of beauty and fascination that one cannot tear oneself away.

People

Beirut has to be, and perhaps always was, one of the world's premier people-watching (or -hearing) sites. Since at least Byzantine times, it has been a refuge for people fleeing political or religious persecution, and in modern ones, it was a

haven for agents and spies such as Kim Philby (the 'Third Man'). Regional turmoil and general globalization combine to create a place where one can meet or at least observe people from almost anywhere, doing almost anything.

A City of Songsters, 1665
Laurent d'Arvieux

All the people of Beirut have good voices and are exceeding fond of singing songs. It is most agreeable to hear them of an evening, singing in their gardens where they are accustomed to eat and drink. They sing at the top of their voice, in the same key, sometimes in several parts, and pitched an octave from each other; they do this with a cup of wine in hand, singing away for up to a quarter of an hour before they raise it to their mouth. This is considered very gallant in the Orient. . . .

Except for the Jews, all the Citizens of Beirut, no matter what their religion, live harmoniously together. They treat each other with courtesy, pay each other visits, and take their entertainment together. The Beirutis are not mean like the inhabitants of Sidon and the other coastal towns; those who live at Tripoli of Syria are more affable still, and their town seems the most like a great city.

An Arab Theater, 1850
David Urquhart

Jan 13th [1850]. After the Megilis [session of court], we went to the Play! The piece, for the opening of the first Arab theatre, was written by the son of one of the members of the Megilis; was to be acted by the family, which was a large one, in their house in the suburbs. They were Maronites and their name Maron. It was curious to find the cognomen of Virgil in this attempt to renovate the Arab muse. The subject announced was "Aroun el Raschid and Jaffer;" the piece was said to be composed in the high Arab style, and interspersed with poetry, which was to be sung. We went on horseback, preceded by blazing fires of rezinous fir, and presently arrived, by a narrow lane and a steep stair (at least for horses), at a house all in disorder, and a crowd of people in all commotion.

When we were introduced into the reception apartments, who should we find there but three grave Ulemas

[Islamic scholars], the two Muftis [Muslim religious authorities] and the Cadi [Chief Islamic Judge]! The room was strewed with roses, lights blazed in all directions; we were overpowered with expressions of gratitude, and served with hot sherbet of cinnamon.

The theatre was in front of the house itself; which was exactly what we seek to imitate by our scenes. There was in the centre a door, on each side of it two windows, and two above; the wings were the advanced part of the court with side doors. The stage was a raised platform in front. The audience was in the court, protected by sails spread over. They had seen in Europe footlights and prompter's box, and fancied it an essential point of theatricals to stick them on where they were not required. In like manner they introduced chairs for the Caliph and his Vizir, and cheval glasses for the ladies. As to costume there was the design at least of observing the proprieties; and, as regards the women, that is the boys dressed up as such, with perfect success. As there were no women on the stage, so were there none in the court, and not even at the windows which opened on the stage.

For Emin Effendi and myself arm-chairs were placed in front, and a large sofa on the left for the judges; the other guests of distinction were on the right, ample space being allowed for the service of pipes and narghillés. Between the acts we retired to the *divan hané*, where refreshments were served; and, though it was long, no one went away, and every one seemed content and merry. Frequent applauses rewarded the author and the actors; and at the close Jaffer, to act the part to the life, threw handfuls of coins amongst us, on which the stage was assailed from all sides with showers of roses.

The curtain after being dropped, was raised again, not because the audience called on a favourite performer, but for the performers to come forward to salute and thank the audience.

A short farce occupied the interval between the second and third acts. It was a husband befooled by his wife, a very grave case, and the ex-Mufti judged it to be so; taking the most vivid interest in the progress, and repeatedly informing the one party of the proceedings of the other. In fact he identified himself with the action, somewhat in the fashion of the ancient chorus, bewailing or approving. The husband at last is undeceived, by observing from the window at the side the lady and her lover; while the Mufti from the *Stalle d'Orchestre* commented vigorously on the guilty nature of the proceedings of the one, and the extreme imbecility of the other. The roars of laughter which these cross-purposes produced conferred on the farce unbounded success, which all were agreed to attribute to the actor whose part the author had not inserted.

A Stroll at Siesta-Time, 1851
Gérard de Nerval

I thought of all this as I went on foot to Beyrouth, about that time of day when, as the Italians say, nobody is to be seen out in the broad sunlight but *gli cani e gli Francesi* [dogs and Frenchmen]. Now this saying, so far as the dogs are concerned, has always seemed untrue to me, for when the hour of the siesta comes, the dogs are always ready enough to stretch themselves idly in the shade and are in no hurry to get a sunstroke. But a Frenchman!

Try to keep him on a divan or a rug the moment after any sort of business, desire, or even simple curiosity has entered his head. The demon of the South seldom weighs heavily upon his chest, and it is not for him that the shapeless Smarra rolls the yellow eyeballs in his great dwarf's head.

So I crossed the plain at that hour which the peoples of the South consecrate to the siesta and the Turks to the *kief* [relaxing with a pipe]. A man who wanders in such a way, when everybody is asleep, in the East runs a serious risk of exciting the same suspicions as a nocturnal vagabond would do with us; but the sentinels on the Fakardin tower only watched me with that compassionate attention which a soldier on watch accords to a belated passer-by. . . .

I had never gone into Beyrouth at this undue hour before, and I felt like that man in *The Thousand and One Nights* who went into a city of the magi, the people of which were turned into stone. Everybody was asleep: the sentinels at the gate; the donkeymen waiting for the ladies in the square; and the ladies themselves probably in the upper galleries of the bath; the date and melon sellers near the fountain; the *cafedji* and all his customers in the cafe; the *hamal,* or porter, with his head resting on his load; the camel-driver beside his kneeling camel, and the tall devils of Albanians who formed the bodyguard before the Pasha's seraglio—all were sleeping the sleep of innocence, leaving the town abandoned.

But in Beyrouth the European colony does not surrender itself completely to the pleasures of the siesta. As I walked toward the right, I soon noticed a certain animation in a street that leads to the square. The penetrating odor of something frying revealed the neighborhood of a trattoria, and the sign of the famous Battista soon met my eyes. I was only too well acquainted with the type of those hotels which, in the Orient, are intended for European travelers and would not have dreamed of taking advantage of the hospitality of Master Battista, the only Frank among the innkeepers of Beyrouth. The English have spoiled these places everywhere, and they are usually far more modest in their accommodation than in their prices.

Lands of the Past, 1876
Viscount de Vogüé

As night fell, we went and sat down in a small cafe on the Beirut square: quite a few idlers, lower-class people—carters, camel-drivers, merchants, all waiting as patiently as statues, each with his hubble-bubble loaded up, for sunset. We are in Ramdhan, the Moslem Lent, and the Prophet's stern law forbids any Moslem from partaking of any food—including tobacco—before the end of the day. The Moslem abides rigorously by this stricture; like all Orientals, whatever their religion, he is strictly obedient with respect to external, material behaviour. No sooner has the sunset cannon freed them, however, than the poor believers take a deep drag of tombac: even after a fourteen-hour fast, they need to smoke even more than they need to eat. . . .

What makes these people strong—and dangerous—is that they are extraordinarily inclined towards religious activity; in Syria, everything starts there. In our old Europe, where religious feeling is more and more diluted, it is hard to imagine how deeply it takes hold of one, penetrating your being, in this alternative moral universe. It must be in the air: in all of its forms, it is inextricably involved in all activities of social life, it sums up the national aspirations of these numerous groups, each so set in its ways, which make up Oriental society. Religion is the only public outlet for their regrets, dissatisfactions, and ambitions, its intrinsic strength is reinforced by those terrible forces. . . .

However, one should not see all their commotions as tragic, or read too much into their verbal histrionics. In this country, a gunshot is gaily called a "war," and a knife-thrust a "massacre."

Evening Promenades, 1878
Gabriel Charmes

If you want to see the high society of Beirut in all its glory, you have to stroll down the Damascus Road, both the Champs-Elysées and Bois de Boulogne of the city, on a feast-day. The present Governor of Lebanon, Rustem Pasha, has planted a small English garden a short distance from the road; this has become the meeting-place for elegant members of both sexes. At first, one reached this miniature but beautifully located garden by crossing Beirut River on a monumental bridge which, naturally, was washed away by the first flood; nowadays, one reaches it by a mere wooden walkway.

The Lebanese militia band produces music to deafen the least delicate ears, while the Pasha, seated under a kiosk in false wood, facing a bed of geraniums or petunias, greets the lovely ladies of the town, making them the most syrupy compliments. This is his manner of proving that he has Christian manners and thus is worthy to govern the Lebanon. Even more interesting than this spectacle are the groups of Syrian women wrapped in their brightly-colored dresses, which one spies here and there among the greenery. They come with their *narghileh*, some fruits and vegetables, and spend the day absorbed in watching and being seen by the passers-by.

Once one has had enough of Rustem Pasha's garden, which does not take long, one goes to sit in one of the small cafes which border the road, munching lettuce washed down with *raki*, smoking a *narghileh*, or just watching the parade of strollers. The riders strut their stuff alongside the carriages, then gather in a clearing in the pine-grove to make one of those displays of Arab horsemanship I never get tired of watching. They gallop along full-speed, throwing a pole that resembles a lance, stop abruptly and wheel their horses towards each other with impressive bravery and grace, then, just before the collision, wheel off as fast as lightning in the other direction.

As for the carriages, that's where you can see the splendid beauties of Beirut, got up in supposedly European style which at first shocks then amuses one. The Christians are turned out in what they imagine is the latest Paris fashion; the Muslim ladies seek to imitate them, but at least have preserved the veil behind which one's not yet cynical imagination can dream of unseen, mysterious charms.

Customs and Fashion

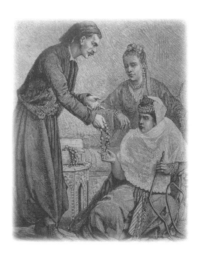

The Beirut souks were not in living memory anything like as colorful as those of Aleppo or Istanbul. However they had perennity: during the archaeological investigations following the 1975–90 Civil War, Byzantine mosaics were found advertising a jeweler's shop . . . under the remains

of the modern Jewelry Souk. Unfortunately, reconstruction has turned the site into a shopping mall where one can find Dolce & Gabbana sunglasses but nary an aubergine. The souks were always the prime vantage point for people-watching, including glimpses of Lebanon's legendary beauties—as some of our travelers, from Gerard de Nerval to Mark Twain, seem to have noticed.

The Tantour, 1850
David Urquhart

On turning the angle of a house, I came upon half a dozen girls and women, flouncing down the rocks, towering with their Tantours, the height of which pronounced them to be of highest caste. Their ponderous and clanking ornaments swept the ground; their white veils blowing out like flags, exposed blooming and laughing faces, and heads which were heaped cornucopias of gems and flowers; necks like the idols of Indian temples, yellow with sparkling gold, and robes of a brown-red, spangled all over with stars, and fringed with lace of the same metal. I was riveted to the spot with the sudden apparition;

they recalled their truant veils, and after a burst of merriment, they bounded past, not caring altogether to shroud either their charms or their finery, and turning again and again, to enjoy or invite my admiration.

What a wonderful custom, this appendage, fixed on the head on the wedding day, remaining there till death, in sleep, in labour of the household, toil in the field, there it sits, knotted and secured, as a bowsprit to the bow of a ship. No superstition belongs to it, no tradition pretends to explain it, no religion consecrates it. . . . It is stuck forward, or a little on one side, the veil resting on it, and on the shoulders, and falling in front, so that it is exactly like a snout: the short ones are about the length of the snout of a well-grown pig. . . . A stranger sight, or a sight of stranger animals, is not to be had within "the four seas." Equally strange the words I am writing will appear fifty years hence, when the Tantour will be but a tradition, and when critics will discover that it never had existence.

Hospitality, 1851
Gérard de Nerval

Syrians still practice religiously the antique virtue of hospitality. You cannot pass by the house of an acquaintance without being practically forced to come in. They insist so pressingly that refusal is impossible. They place you in the place of honor on the sofa, they bring you pipes; then slaves bring you coffee in tiny cups held in finely worked gold or silver *zarfs* [cup-holders] which protect your fingers from the heat. If you are especially familiar with the master of the house, the ladies favor you with their presence; they will personally offer you the sherbet or jams, then will remain in the sitting-room without their veils, allowing you to examine their beautiful features and sumptuous clothing at your leisure.

They wear wide pantaloons closed above the ankle; this first garment is covered by a long robe open in the front, with a brightly-colored silk scarf worn as a belt, or by a shawl in Indian cashmere. Then comes a tightly-fitting vest all embroidered with gold thread, with narrow sleeves open up to the elbow; the sheerness of their gauze blouses leaves their breasts discreetly visible. Their hair, plaited in a myriad of braids, falls down their backs in tresses which they augment with matching-colored braids of silk, studded with gold coins and held straight by the weight of rings. They wear a tiny bonnet in red wool, embroidered with gold, with a fat gold tassel, coquettishly fastened atop their heads. Their eyebrows and eyelashes are carefully dyed black. The nails and palms of their hands are inevitably dyed with henna to a reddish-brown, unappetizing hue; many of them wear makeup as well.

Beauties of Beirut, 1869
Mark Twain

The rest of us had nothing to do but look at the beautiful city of Beirout, with its bright, new houses nestled among a wilderness of green shrubbery spread abroad over an upland that sloped gently down to the sea; and also at the mountains of Lebanon that environ it; and likewise to bathe in the transparent blue water that rolled its billows about the ship (we did not know there were sharks there.) We had also to range up and down through the town and look at the costumes. These are picturesque and fanciful, but not so varied as at Constantinople and Smyrna; the women of Beirout add an agony—in the two former cities the sex wear a thin veil which one can see through (and they often expose their ankles), but at Beirout they cover their entire faces with dark-colored or black veils, so that they look like mummies, and then expose their breasts to the public.

Types and Costumes, 1878
Gabriel Charmes

Strolling around Beirut, one admires the varied and fantastical costumes of the Arabs, the noble bearing of the Druzes wrapped in their *abayas* as in an antique toga, the proud allure of the Damascene sheikhs, the proud carriage and splendid rags of the Bedouins, the processions of emirs from the mountain, the multicolored robes of the clergy of every community, the loose trousers and elegant turbans of the city-dwellers, in a word: the mixture of dress, communities, races, and conditions, of physical looks and colors, which one finds everywhere in the East, but nowhere as abundantly as in Syria. Seated in front of the cafes, you see a variegated crowd, loafers, camel-drivers, bourgeois, merchants, simple louts, all smoking the *narghileh* or eating a salad with the charming gravity with which the Orientals deal with the simplest aspects of life.

The Bazaar, 1838
Edouard Blondel

This is the liveliest quarter of the town, reminding one of a magic lantern where the scene changes all the time. One could not find a better vantage point to study the physical types and varied costumes of the country. Priests, dervishes, bedouins from the desert, peasants from Mount Lebanon, Druzes, Egyptians, black women and slaves of all kinds, all coming and going, crowding and jostling each other from every direction. . . .

The only shops of any interest are those of the silk merchants, selling local wares. Having observed the crudely constructed looms they use, one is astonished by the beautiful cloth they produce. In previous times, the whole population used to dress in silks; since the Egyptian occupation, everything has changed. Burdened by taxes and levies, they no longer have the means to indulge in such a luxury.

Clothes-Shopping, 1851
Gérard de Nerval

Mountain folk crowded the huge bazaar, which takes up the whole of the centre quarters, and is divided into departments for food-stuffs and merchandise. The presence of women in some of the shops is an unusual thing in the Orient, and is only to be explained by the scarcity of people of Mussulman origin in Beyrouth.

Nothing could be more entertaining than to go through these long rows of stalls, protected by different coloured shades which do not prevent a few rays of the sun from playing upon the fruits and vegetables so marvellously coloured; or, farther on, from making the embroidery sparkle upon the rich garments that hang outside every old clothes shop. I was very anxious to add to my costume an item of adornment which is only found in Syria. This consists in draping the forehead and temples with a gold-striped silk handkerchief, which is called *caffieh*. It is kept on the head by tying around it a string of twisted horsehair, and its purpose is to preserve the ears and neck from the draughts which are so danger- ous in a mountainous country. I was sold a very gorgeous one for forty piastres, and after going to try it on at a barber's, I thought I looked like an Eastern king. . . .

I have never seen such handsome children as those who were running about and playing in the most beau- tiful avenue in the bazaar. Laughing, slender maidens crowded around elegant marble fountains in the Moorish style and, in due time, went away, bearing on their heads large vessels of ancient shape. In this country many red heads are to be seen, whose shade, darker than with us, has something of purple or of scarlet about it. This col- our is considered so beautiful in Syria, that many women tint their fair or black hair with henna, which everywhere else is used only to redden the soles of the feet, the nails and palms of the hands.

There were people selling sherbets and ices at the various places where the lanes meet, making these beverages with snow gathered at the summit of Sannin. A gorgeous cafe at the central point of the bazaar, mainly frequented by soldiers, also supplied iced and perfumed drinks. I stayed there some time, never becoming weary of the movement of this active crowd, which brought together in a single place the varied costumes of the mountains. Besides, there was a certain element of comedy in watching, in the bargaining between buyers and sellers, the balancing of the jewelled cornets, more than a foot high, which the Druse and Maronite women wear upon their heads, and from which there falls over their faces a long veil which they throw back whenever they feel so inclined. The position of this ornament makes them look like the fabulous unicorns which support the royal arms of England. Their outer garments are invariably black or white.

Rites of Passage,
Passing the Time

*The multi-ethnic makeup of Lebanon in general and Beirut
in particular means that the important rites and feasts of life
are done in different ways. It was traditional for Christian*

and Muslim neighbors to pay each other visits on their feast-days, weddings, and funerals, and some of our Travelers found themselves invited to or caught up in such celebrations. Christian or Muslim, the favorite social gathering-place was the hammam, or Turkish bath, still an institution throughout the Middle East. The early European voyagers were astonished at what they saw as an obsession with cleanliness, and rightly identified it with the religious duty of ablutions before prayer. However, the hammam is more than that: a place of relaxation, socializing, an oasis from the hurly-burly of life in the teeming streets of the Levant.

A Christian Wedding, 1832
Alphonse de Lamartine

September 27: Fakardin's Tower. We have passed all the day at the nuptials of the young Syrian-Greek girl. The ceremony commenced by a long procession of Greek, Arab, and Syrian women, who came, some on horseback, others on foot, through the roads of aloes and mulberries, to assist the bride during this fatiguing day. For several days and nights a certain number of these women has never left Habib's house, nor ceased to utter shrill and prolonged cries, songs, and groans, similar to those shouts which the reapers and haymakers make on the coasts of France during the harvests. These clamours, lamentations, tears, and rejoicings, must prevent the bride from getting any sleep for several nights before the marriage. The old and young men of the family of the husband make as many on their side, and permit him scarcely any repose for eight days beforehand.

Introduced into the gardens of Habib's house, the females were made to enter into the interior of the divan, to pay their compliments to the young girl, to admire her dress, and to see the ceremonies. As for us, we were left in the court, or called into an outer room. There a table was laid out in the European manner, covered with a multitude of dried fruits, honey, and sugar-cakes, liquors, and sherbet; and during the evening they renewed these refreshments, as the numerous visitors exhausted them. I succeeded in being admitted as an exception into the divan of the women, at the moment when the Greek archbishop was bestowing the nuptial benediction. The

young girl was standing up by the side of the bridegroom, covered from head to foot with a veil of red
gauze, embroidered with gold. The priest lifted up the
veil for a moment, and the young man for the first time
got a glimpse of her to whom he was uniting his fate;
she was extremely pretty. The paleness which fatigue and
emotion spread upon her cheeks was rendered yet more
striking by the reflection of the red veil, and the count-
less ornaments of gold, silver, pearls, and diamonds with
which she was covered, and by the long tresses of her jet-
black hair which fell around her person. This, joined to
her eyelashes painted black, as well as her eyebrows, and
the margins of her eyes, her hands, with the tips of her
fingers and nails, stained red with henna, and marked
with Moorish designs, all gave to her ravishing beauty a
character of novelty and solemnity with which we were
singularly struck.

Her husband had scarcely time to see her. He appeared
exhausted, and fainting under the infliction of the vigils
and fatigues with which these ridiculous customs extin-
guish even the force of love. The prelate took from the

hands of one of his priests a chaplet of natural flowers, placed it on the head of the young girl, took it off, put it on the hair of the youth, again took it off, to set it on the veil of the bride, and thus passed it several times from one head to the other. Then he put, in the same alternate manner, rings on the fingers of both. They afterwards broke the same piece of bread, they drank the consecrated wine in the same cup. After which they removed the bride into the apartments where women alone could follow her, in order to change her dress. The father and friends of the bridegroom led him into the garden, and made him sit down at the foot of a tree, surrounded by all the males of his family. The musicians and dancers then arrived, and continued till the setting of the sun their barbarous symphonies, their piercing cries, and their contortions, around the young man, who had sunk into sleep at the foot of the tree, resisting all the efforts of his friends to awaken him. At night they conducted him alone, and in procession, to his father's house. It is not until after eight days that a newly-married husband is permitted to take his wife, and conduct her to his own house.

The women, who filled the house of Habib with their exclamations, also issued forth a little later. Nothing was more picturesque than this prodigious procession of women and young girls, in their strange and splendid costumes, covered with glittering stones, surrounded by their servants and their slaves, bearing torches of resinous pine to lighten the road, and extending thus their luminous train through the long and narrow paths, shaded by aloes and oranges, to the borders of the sea, sometimes in a profound silence, sometimes uttering piercing cries which resounded over the waves, or beneath the large plantains at the foot of Lebanon. We returned to our house, close to the country residence of Habib, where we continued to hear the noise of the women of the family conversing; we mounted upon our terraces, and followed with our eyes for a long time the wandering lights, which danced on all sides through the trees in the plain.

A Muslim Funeral, 1851
Gérard de Nerval

I left the café and walked towards the promenade of Raz-Beyrouth which is on the left of the town. The ruddy glare of the setting sun was tingeing with delightful reflections the mountain chain which goes down to Sidon; on the right, the seashore seemed a mass of rocky openings, with natural pools here and there, left full of water by the Storms. Women and girls were dipping their feet in them as they bathed little children there. Many of those pools seemed like the remains of ancient baths, with marble pavements. On the left, near a little mosque which stands above a Turkish burial-ground, some huge columns of red granite were lying on the earth, and it may be, as people say, that they mark the site of the circus of Herod Agrippa. I was endeavouring to answer this question for myself when I heard songs and sounds of music coming from a ravine that is beside the city walls. I thought it might be a marriage, for the songs were joyful in character; but soon there appeared a group of Mussulmans waving banners, then others who carried on their

shoulders a kind of litter containing a body. Women followed, uttering cries, and then a number of men with
more banners and branches of trees. They all came to a
halt in the graveyard, and laid down the body, completely
covered with flowers. The nearness of the sea gave a kind
of dignity to the scene and even to the impression created
by the strange songs they sang in their droning voices.

Those who were taking the air gathered and watched
the ceremony respectfully. An Italian business-man near
me told me that this was no ordinary funeral; that the
deceased was a holy man who had long lived at Beyrouth, where the Franks regarded him as a madman, but
the Mussulmans as a saint. Recently he had lived in a
grotto under a terrace in one of the gardens of the town,
quite naked, and with the manners of a wild beast, and
people had come from all parts to seek his counsel. From
time to time he made a tour of the town and took everything he thought would be useful to him from the shops
of the Arab merchants. When he did this, the merchants
were full of gratitude, believing that he would bring
them luck; but the Europeans, not sharing this opinion,

had complained to the Pasha after a few visits, and had succeeded in getting a ruling that the holy man should not leave his garden. The Turks, who are not very numerous at Beyrouth, had not objected to this, and contented themselves with supplying the holy man with provisions and presents. Now this personage was dead and the people showed every sign of joy, for a Turkish saint is not to be mourned in the manner of an ordinary mortal. The certainty that after so many acts of penance he has finally attained to everlasting happiness causes this event to be regarded as a happy one, and it is celebrated to the sound of music. In other days there used to be dancing, singing and public banquets in such a case.

Ladies' Day at the Bath, 1832
Alphonse de Lamartine

September 19. To-day my wife and Julia have been invited, by the wife and daughter of a neighbouring Arab chief, to pass the day in the bath; it is the amusement of the women of the East amongst themselves. A bath is announced fifteen days beforehand, as a ball in

Europe. The following is the description of this festival, as given us by my wife in the evening:—The bath-rooms are in a public place, to which the approach of men is prohibited every day up to a certain hour, in order to keep them exclusively for the women, and the whole day when the bath is required for a bride, as was the case on the present occasion. The rooms are feebly lighted, through small domes of painted glass. They are paved with marble, in compartments of different colours, worked with great art. The walls are also covered with marble in mosaic, or adorned with mouldings or Moorish pillars. The rooms are graduated as to heat; the first of the temperature of the outer air, the second lukewarm, the others successively hotter, until the last, where the steam, from water nearly boiling, rises from basins, and fills the air with its stifling heat. In general, there is not a hollow bath in the centre of the room; there are only spouts always flowing, which pour on the marble floor about half an inch of water. This water escapes by channels, and is incessantly renewed. What is called the bath in the East is not a complete immersion, but a succession of sprinklings more or less hot, and the pressing of vapour on the skin.

Two hundred ladies of the town and the neighbourhood were invited this day to the bath, and in the number several young European females; each arrived enveloped in the immense cloak of white linen, which entirely covers the superb costume of the women when they leave home. They were all accompanied by their black slaves or free servants: as they arrived, they formed into groups, and seated themselves on the mats and cushions prepared in the first vestibule; their attendants removed the cloak which encompassed them, and they appeared in all the rich and picturesque magnificence of their clothes and jewels. These costumes are greatly varied in the colour of the stuffs, and the number and splendour of the jewels, but they are uniform in the shape of the garments. These garments consist of pantaloons with large folds of streaked satin, bound at the waist by a tissue of red silk, and closed round the ankle by a band of gold or silver; a loose robe, worked in gold, open in front, and tied under the breast, which it leaves uncovered; the sleeves are tight from the shoulder, and hang loose from the elbow to the wrist; beneath is a chemise of silken gauze passing over the bosom.

Above their robe they wear a vest of scarlet velvet, lined with ermine or marten, embroidered with gold at all the seams, and the sleeves open. The hair is parted at the crown of the head; one part falls down over the neck, the rest is twisted into tresses with black silk resembling the hair, and descends to the feet. Little wreaths of gold or silver hang at the extremity of these tresses, and by their weight draw them down the full length of the figure; on their heads small strings of pearls, of golden sequins, and of natural flowers, are scattered, the whole mixed together with incredible profusion. It seems as if the contents of a casket had been thrown at hazard upon the brilliant hair, so redolent is it in jewels and flowers. This barbaric luxury has the most picturesque effect upon young girls of fifteen to twenty years of age. On the top of the head some women wear a cap of carved gold, in the form of an inverted cup; from the middle of this cap a string of gold, with a row of pearls, hangs pendant down the back. The legs are unadorned, and the feet are covered with yellow slippers, which they drag as they walk. The arms are crowded with bracelets of gold, silver, and pearls; the breast with several necklaces, which shield the uncovered bosom with chains of gold or pearls.

When all the ladies were collected, a barbarous music was heard; women whose bodies were clothed in a simple red gauze uttered sharp and doleful cries, and played on the fife and tambourine. This concert never ceased throughout the day, and imparted to a scene of pleasure and rejoicing a character of uproar and frenzy perfectly savage. When the bride appeared, accompanied by her mother and her young friends, attired in a costume so magnificent, that her hair, neck, arms, and bosom were entirely concealed under a floating veil of garlands, gold, and pearls, the bathing-women seized her, and took off, piece by piece, all her garments. During this process the other females were undressed by their slaves, and the different ceremonies of the bath commenced. They passed from one saloon to another, always to the sound of the same music, and always with the most absurd ceremonies and words. They took the vapour-bath; then the water bath; then they had thrown over them perfumed soap water. At length the sports began, and all the ladies, with various gestures and cries, gambolled like a troop of schoolboys taken to bathe in a stream, splashing each other, plunging their heads into the water, and throwing it upon their bodies; and the music struck up with an increased roar every time that any of these infantine tricks excited the noisy laughter of the young Arab girls.

At length they left the bath; the slaves and servants twisted afresh the damp hair of their mistresses, arranged again the necklaces and bracelets, put on the silken robes and velvet vests, stretched the cushions on the mats in the rooms where they had dried the floors, and drew from baskets and silk coverings the provisions brought for the collation. They consisted of pastry and sweetmeats of all kinds, in which the Turks and Arabs excel; sherbet, orange-flowers, and all the iced drinks of which the Orientals make use at every moment of the day. Pipes and hookahs were brought for the elder females; a cloud of odoriferous smoke filled and obscured the atmosphere;

coffee, served in little cups, enclosed in small open vases of gold or silver thread, never ceased circulating, and conversation became animated. Then followed the dancing-girls, who executed, to the sounds of the same music, the Egyptian dances and the monotonous evolutions of Arabia. The whole day was thus passed, and it was not till the fall of night that this cortege of women reconducted the young affianced bride to the house of her mother. This ceremony of the bath usually takes place a few days before marriage.

The Hammam, 1854
R.P. Laorty-Hadji

The greatest pleasure of both men and women is the bath, the oriental bath which has nothing in common with ours except the name. In the Orient, baths are like Greek and Roman spas with even more sensual refinements. . . .

Don't come here looking for oval European-style bathtubs or basins hollowed out in the rock. The oriental bath consists merely of being sprayed and dipped, vats and showers. The bather never enters a vessel full of water;

instead, supine on the marble, he lies immobile, wrapped in this fragrant cloud which slowly penetrates his very pores. Gradually, his body opens up to this unwonted temperature; a gentle moisture slowly leaves his skin, the sinews relax, the arms and legs go soft. After this first impression, the bath-house servants come and take hold of the bather, who is stretched out on a thin mat, his head resting on a cushion, abandoning his limp body. The servant massages the flesh, makes the joints crack, and then puts on a horse-hair glove with which he energetically rubs the whole body with it, bringing the circulation practically to the boil under the skin. This rub-down, this massage, which takes the European by surprise, is one of the more delightful moments of the oriental bath.

When it's over, one feels completely vague and listless. Were this to continue for long, it might be dangerous. So before long, one leaves, much as one does our steam-baths or hot mineral waters, leaving the scalding atmosphere to pass through the various rooms one came through on the way in. In one of these rooms, the attendant comes up with tepid water which he showers over the shoulders, along with a soapy foam and rose-water to perfume the body; finally he leaves the bather reclining on a divan, where aromatic tobacco, coffee, and sherbets restore his strength. The bath lasts several hours, and is the Muslim's great pastime. Besides the pleasure of the experience, it is a religious duty. Turkish women find in the bath the only distraction allowed them in their seclusion: they discuss their personal business, baptisms, dances and marriages. Men are banned from the bath-house during women's hours, but when it is their turn, they congregate as if at a club, to hold forth on political and business affairs.

The French Connection

France was one of the first European countries to cultivate commercial relations with the Ottoman Empire, signing the famous "Capitulations" treaty that gave France priority rights to trade in Ottoman ports. The French soon extended this to a role as protector of certain Catholic populations in the Levant, notably the Maronites. By the beginning of the twentieth century, French missionary schools were educating a large proportion of the Christian and a non-negligible number of Muslim children in Lebanon and Syria. Most of the educated Christians, and many Muslims, are still bilingual or at least conversant in French.

French Education for Girls and Boys, 1878
Gabriel Charmes

The Jesuit establishment in Beirut, known as the Saint Joseph University, sits in the very center of the town, so as to be visible from everywhere. Few of our [French] lycées could compete with this college. It offers every aspect of hygiene and comfort which our own schools and colleges lack. . . . A chapel, decorated with a double row of marble columns (that secular art which the Jesuits are adept at decorating their churches with) receives the college's three hundred fifty children as well as the five or six hundred trooped there from the nearby schools of the Sisters of Saint Joseph. Every Sunday, a thousand or so of the Latin Rite faithful take to coming to the Jesuits and leave the church of their own community. There is primary and secondary education, as well as a seminary for the clergy of different rites; there will soon be a medical school as well. . . .

In Beirut, keen attention is paid to the education of girls as well as boys. The Sisters of Saint Joseph, the Sisters of Saint Vincent of Paul, and the Nazareth order maintain convents which cater to all classes of society. . . . Hundreds of young girls receive a perfectly adequate education: they learn to read, write, count, and sew. I was very pleased on visiting their classes; you see little girls of all sects and nationalities. When a man enters, the Turks turn towards the wall, but I noticed them stealing glances sideways, which allowed me to see their round and pale faces, so different from the dusky, elongated faces of the Arabs. Many of the nuns are natives. . . . The "Birds" Convent is an exceedingly luxurious gothic edifice, set in the middle of a superb park which affords a splendid panoramic vista. The young girls who are brought up there belong to the highest society of Syria. They are taught all kinds of useful things and many superfluous ones: grammar and mythology, history and botany, physics and archaeology, not to mention music and proper manners which occupy an important place in the curriculum.

Orientals in general, and Syrians in particular, have a strong tendency to become fancy-talking lawyers or men of letters; there is no need to develop their penchant for poetry or eloquence. If one day this country obtains its independence, I fear that it will escape from the hands of the Turks only to fall under the tutelage of some European Power. Government and administration will not provide a significant amount of employment to the natives of the country; a preparation for industry is the best thing for them: their commercial aptitude, their genius for business is what should be developed.

A Levantine Investigation, 1914
Maurice Barrès

First Sight of Beirut. Beirut gives such a sweet impression, with the little whitish or greyish squares of its houses with their gently pointed roofs, the red tiles so harmonious amid the greenery. I shall never forget this heat, this humidity, the mist that seems to wrap around us. . . . I breathed the odor of Asia. . . .

I am not confining myself to the great premises of the Saint Joseph University. Each day, from morning until night, I criss-cross Beirut: to the Brothers of Christian Doctrine, the Daughters of Charity, the Sisters of Nazareth, and those of Saint Joseph; or to the French Lay

Mission, or to the Jews. That is to say, everywhere one is safe from the enemy, the American Protestants. . . .

The danger is that we are bringing up a young generation of misfits: uprooted, idle, discontented, always shooting off in the direction of political, social, and religious reforms. The graduate, enough of a troublemaker in the West, full of hatred for a society that fails to provide him with a position commensurate with his expectations, becomes in the Islamic World a Young Turk, Young Egyptian, or Young Tunisian. . . .

A young man came to see me, and said: "I am the son and grandson of official dragomans. My grandfather met Lamartine and Saulcy; we have a number of letters from them. How do you find our country?"

"Very beautiful indeed."

"Beautiful?!" he exclaimed, horrified.

I led him to the window and pointed to Lebanon, Mount Sannin covered with snow, those peaks reaching up towards the infinity of Heaven. "It is impossible to live here," he said. "You wish to come to Paris?" All the young people of this country, he said, would like to go there. . . .

At the end of the meal, a charming boy was brought in, the son of Mr Tobia [of Aamchit, where Renan wrote and where his sister Henriette died and is buried]. Off we go to see the house where Renan lived, and meet the boy's father who remembers well having met him. As we walk, we chat, the boy and I. "Your country is so beautiful: I cannot recall ever having seen a more beautiful one."

"Ah!" he said. "When Monsieur Vedrines [French aviator] passed by, up in the sky, he slowed down his flight as he passed over here." I was greatly moved by what he had said: how proud this charming little chap is of his country, and how happily he associates the idea of heaven with the idea of France!

Americans Abroad

Americans were slow to join the bandwagon of pilgrimage and Grand Tour travel to the Levant, but once they did they published prolific memoirs and began a dynamic missionary activity, providing schools and hospitals throughout the Ottoman Empire. One catalyst for American involvement was the Syrian Protestant College, a missionary-founded educational institution in Beirut that soon became—in its modern guise as the American University of Beirut—the foremost university in the Levant.

American Missionaries, 1878
Gabriel Charmes

The number of Protestants has been increasing steadily, drawn by proselytizing that does not only address itself to the soul. The Americans are the most ardent of such proselytizers. It would be absurd to accuse them of political motives in their policy: there is nothing more disinterested than the propaganda they diffuse with such energy. However, one has to admit that the new converts are especially drawn to the English protection that comes with conversion, and this accounts for a good part of the American pastors' success. Syrians would be quite reluctant to become Protestant if America were the only Protestant one of the Great Powers. They seek protection in their choice of religion, which America is too far away to provide. But England is there and only too glad to take advantage of the American good works. Thus Protestantism has made rapid progress, bringing with it a civilizing element as well as one more cause of discord among all those already fermenting in Syria. . . .

What we call higher education is represented in Beirut by the Protestant American university whose vast campus, located on the edge of town, is a model of sound construction, elegance, and cleanliness; I emphasize this last quality, so rare in the East, and to which the Protestants are particularly attached. The smallest village schools are as carefully run as comparable schools in England or in America. As for the American University of Beirut, situated at the edge of town in its magnificent garden which goes all the way down to the sea, its material standards rival those of any establishment in France. The precinct of the University dominates the Gulf of Beirut, the view from there affording a magnificent panorama. . . .

The courses at the University embrace both letters and sciences; but they especially focus on medicine. Since the American missions are especially keen on making converts, it is only natural that they concentrate on training doctors whose influence in the countryside is even greater in the East than in Europe. The teaching is both theoretical and practical, and they have founded hospitals which run excellent clinics.

While I was living in Beirut, they used to teach all their courses in Arabic, which in my opinion did a signal service to that language, ill-adapted as it is to scientific purposes. Now they have changed and teach in English; it seems that the Governor of Lebanon, Rustem Pasha, put a lot of pressure on them to give up teaching in Arabic, in the hope that the progress of English would one day overtake the dominance of French. They were sorely misguided in following the advice of Rustem Pasha. They had done more than anyone for the progress of civilization in Syria, not just by teaching in Arabic, but by publishing in that language a series of scientific works which were thus made available to the indigenous people. . . . All branches of study are pursued; medicine, as I mentioned, attracts the most students, leading as it does to a stable career, a must to the practical mind of the Syrians.

A Difficult Language, 1910
Henry Jessup

The Arabic language . . . is a burden at first, but the Master, while He does not require us to love the burden, does tell us to love to bear it. Every missionary ought to try most earnestly to love the language through which he is to preach the Gospel of Christ to his fellow men, and that, in order that he may learn it well and be able to use it as not abusing it. . . . Correct pronunciation of Arabic is the prime necessity. By mispronunciation a Greek bishop prayed that the Lord would create a clean dog (kelb, instead of kolb, heart) in each of His people. A missionary lady told her servant to put more donkeys in the bread (using "hameer" instead of "khameer," leaven). A missionary calling on the local governor and wishing to thank him for some act of his, said, "I am crazy to Your Excellency" (using "mejnoon" instead of "memnoon," obliged). Similar instances might be multiplied indefinitely—notably Dr. Dennis' funeral sermon in which by a mispronunciation of K, he confused "trials" with "roosters" to the mystification of the mourners.

Commercial Instinct, 1869
Mark Twain

A young gentleman (I believe he was a Greek,) volunteered to show us around the city, and said it would afford him great pleasure, because he was studying

English and wanted practice in that language. When we had finished the rounds, however, he called for remuneration—said he hoped the gentlemen would give him a trifle in the way of a few piastres (equivalent to a few five cent pieces.) We did so. The Consul was surprised when he heard it, and said he knew the young fellow's family very well, and that they were an old and highly respectable family and worth a hundred and fifty thousand dollars! Some people, so situated, would have been ashamed of the berth he had with us and his manner of crawling into it.

An Easy Place to Govern? 1861
Henry Jessup

July 18th [1861] Daud Pasha was inaugurated as governor-general of the new *pashalic* [governorate] of Mount Lebanon. The ceremony took place in Beirut barracks, the *firman* of appointment was read in Turkish and Arabic, and addresses were made by Maronite and Greek priests. . . . Daud Pasha had a difficult role. He had not only to reckon with the animosities of the old feudal sheikhs and peasantry, but to circumvent the intrigues and secret schemes of the Philo-Russian Greeks, the Philo-French Maronites, the Philo-English Druses, and the Philo-Turk Moslems. Lebanon is easy to govern if left to itself. The great peril after the initial trial of the new order of government by Daud Pasha was not from Zahleh or Deir el Komr, but from Paris and St. Petersburg.

The Modern Metropolis

Beirut's rise from sleepy red-roofed village to teeming metropolis began in the mid-nineteenth century and was complete by the mid-twentieth. The dual assault by development and population growth that turned a charming town nestled in

an enchanting natural setting into a sprawling concrete and high-rise megapolis did not fail to impress our travelers.

Beirut's Bright Future, 1851
Gérard de Nerval

I went and sat down in a cafe, built upon a kind of dais supported as upon piles by pillars driven into the seashore. Through the cracks in the planks I could see the greenish water beating on the shore beneath my feet. Sailors of every country, mountaineers, Bedouins in their white robes, Maltese and a few piratical looking Greeks, smoke and chat around me; two or three young *cafedjis* [*waiters*] stand by and occasionally refill with a foaming mokka the *finjanes* [cups] in their holders of gilded filigree. Here and there, the sun, as it goes down over the mountains of Cyprus, just beyond the extreme edge of the waves, lights up the picturesque embroideries which sparkle even on the poorest of rags; it draws attention to the immense shadow of the castle which protects the harbour to the right of the jetty; it is a mass of towers grouped upon the rocks, and its walls were breached and holed by the English bombardment of 1840. Now it is nothing more than a ruin held together only by its mass, a witness to the iniquity of futile destructiveness. On the left, a pier goes out into the sea with the white buildings of the customs upon it. Like the harbour itself, it is almost entirely built out of the remains of columns from the ancient Beryta or the Roman city of Julia Felix.

Will Beyrouth ever again behold the splendours which thrice have made her queen of the Lebanon? Today her situation at the foot of verdant mountains, in the middle of fertile plains and gardens, at the end of a delightful gulf which is continually crowded with the ships of Europe; the Damascus trade, and the fact that she is a central meeting-place for the industrious peoples of the mountain, give Beyrouth her power and her prospects for the future.

Mainstream of Progress, 1854
R.P. Laorty-Hadji

Today Beirut is in the mainstream of progress. This fortunate disposition is without doubt to be attributed to the influence of Western pilgrims and merchants who constantly flock there. Beirut has become the most important town on the coast, the hub for all the commerce of Syria. Its port is extremely secure, and constantly full of shipping. In the city one can find every convenience of life, dwellings which are nearly comfortable, healthy meats, delicious fruits, bread baked in European style by Frankish bakers, delicious and inexpensive wines, among others, the famous "golden wine"—the king of wine, much vaunted in the East, where it is as popular as our Champagne in France, and indeed theirs is also sparkling. But one of the reasons for Beirut's reputation is the unique beauty of its surroundings, the magnificent mulberry groves which overlook the city from all sides. Then there is the picturesque aspect of its antique ruins lying about among the flowers, and especially the gracious villas scattered by the hundreds among the lemon-trees, prickly-pears, carob-trees and other trees of all sorts which grow there. In a word, Beirut still deserves the name of "happy" with which the Emperor Augustus gratified it.

Beirut Modernizes, 1863
Henry Jessup

The first telegraphic despatch went through from Beirut to Constantinople February 1, 1863. The Moslems were filled with wonder and say it is a pity that Mohammed did not know it, as, had he known of it, all the world would have gone after him. Nor was Beirut unworthy of being ushered into the society of Europe. In 1823 it had 6,000 population; in 1840, 10,000; in 1856, 22,000, and in 1863, 70,000. Seven lines of European steamers touched at Beirut and the streets of Beirut were being widened and macadamized to allow the carriages of the French Damascus Road Company to pass.

Epitome of the East, 1905
Gertrude Bell

Beyrout, 18 January, 1905. I'm deep in the gossip of the East! It's so enjoyable. I thought to-day when I was strolling through the bazaars buying various odds and ends what a pleasure it was to be in the East almost as part of it, to know it all as I know Syria now, to be able to

tell from the accent of the people where they come from
and exchange the proper greeting as one passes. A bazaar
is always the epitome of the East, even in a half European town like Beyrout. I also went to the big mosque
and photographed the doors which are rather pretty and
made friends with the Imams—great fun it was! I feel a
very fine fellow now that I am the lord of two horses.

A Place to Be Reckoned With, 1918
T.E. Lawrence

*For Lawrence, Lebanon was too frenchified, not Arab
enough to be of interest . . .*

Beyrout was altogether new. It would have been bas-
tard French in feeling as in language but for its Greek
harbour and American college. Public opinion in it was
that of the Greek merchants, fat men living by exchange;
for Beyrout itself produced nothing. The next strongest
component was the class of returned emigrants, happy
on invested savings in the town of Syria which most

resembled that Washington Avenue where they had made good. Beyrout was the door of Syria, a chromatic Levantine screen through which cheap or shop-soiled foreign influences entered; it represented Syria as much as Soho the Home Counties.

Yet Beyrout, because of its geographical position, because of its schools, and the freedom engendered by intercourse with foreigners, had contained before the war a nucleus of people, talking, writing, thinking like the doctrinaire Cyclopaedists who paved the way for revolution in France. For their sake, and for its wealth, and its exceeding loud and ready voice, Beyrout was to be reckoned with.

Constant Yet Changeable, 1946
Robin Fedden

For most travellers Beirut is their first contact with Syria and the Lebanon, and beautiful it seems to one coming in by boat. The mountains climb tier upon tier into a blue sky, olive groves encircle the town with a belt of soft grey, and to the south of the promontory on which Beirut is so comfortably placed, spread orange sand-hills dotted with clumps of umbrella pine. Seen from the sea, the palms with which the town is sprinkled appear to sprout mysteriously from the very stone, and there is an impression of gaiety and colour in the quays and houses that crowd along the foreshore; while down the coast stretch pleasant bays where the waves break lazily on the sand and coves invite the bather. The gaiety and the colour do not disappear as you land. The streets are full of movement, and the *suks* are crowded. Stalls display an amazing variety of fruit from the rich hillsides around, and expensive antique shops sell the usual medley of genuine and fake.

In spite of the appalling speculative development that the town has suffered, the natural setting of Beirut never fails to enchant. On some coasts the sea ends abruptly, defined and terminated by the shore. Not so here. It is almost as if the Mediterranean, grudging the strip of green between its waves and the mountains, extended its influence inland. From every window you look out to sea, from every orchard and olive grove through wreaths of leaves you glimpse the blue. The warm sea air washes in lazy tides across the cultivation to the mountains' feet and excites the narrow coastal fringe to lush bewildering growth. Hibiscus, acacia, huge overgrown sunflowers, and the towers of grey-green eucalyptus that line the roads outside Beirut, bathe in the tidal air. No seed falls but it sprouts; and they are, in a sense, sea crops that the overloaded donkey-carts ferry into the town. Above, the mountains climb, deliberate and stair-like, steadily away from the sea's encroachment into the high clear air. Overhanging Beirut they are as inescapable as the sea.

Constant yet changeable, they are always there yet never twice the same; each change that the day brings to their still flanks and snow-capped summits lifts the eyes with a new surprise and pleasure from the movement of the streets. Even on dark nights they remain present, for the lights of Aley and the mountain villages shine in clusters too emphatic to be mistaken for stars. Under a full moon the nine-thousand-foot snows of Sannine positively throb with light and hang so deceptively close that it seems you could almost stretch out your hand to them, and feel on your forearm the freezing air.

Commercial Ardor, 1946
Robin Fedden

This noble setting contrasts sharply with the *negotiatio-nis ardour* that stirs the town and gives it fevered life. Now that it has abandoned Alexandria, the Spirit of the Levant here makes its capital. Under its jealous rule trade prospers, but much else languishes. It sometimes seems as though only chaffering thrives in the moist sea air. This air, as you drive from the mountains down to Beirut, strikes your windscreen like a mist. Through the heavy and palpable vapour it is impossible to see Beirut for months at a time from the mountains above. A haze envelops the town and its promontory, and creeps even into the foot-hills. The obscurity is symbolic of the change from the ascetic deserts and the mountain villages to the miasmic Levant. Rich and uncertain, heady and oppressive, the air blurs shapes and principles, precludes clarity of action and thought. But it drives trade, it is the heavy fuel on which the Levantine works. Under this haze enterprises spawn and coin turns rapidly. The obscure deal and the close contract burgeon into fortunes.

Any criticism of Beirut is also a criticism of the West, for the town is superficially westernized. Here, however, as elsewhere in the Middle East, though our machines find no difficulty in acclimating themselves, our ideas are not in the same case. Further, though our machines are good, the level of our cultural exports is lamentably low. In the West a lack of taste and shoddy values are sometimes offset by traditional feeling and culture which temper the futility of the time. On the Levantine seaboard Turkish tradition and culture have been swept away pell-mell by the sudden onset of 20th-century technology and its curious novelties. Our machines have uprooted an old culture but have not supplied a new. Beirut is a town without a tradition.

The Writers

LAURENT D'ARVIEUX (1635–1702) was French consul in Algiers and then Aleppo for many years, returning to write his memoirs, which were published posthumously. He knew the area and its languages intimately, and was perhaps the first westerner to leave a deeply informed (if not unprejudiced) account of the region and its customs.

KARL BAEDEKER (1801–59) was a German publisher who founded a company that commissioned and published very detailed guides to various countries, including Syria and Palestine (modern Syria, Lebanon, Israel, and Palestine).

JOANNES BARBUCALLUS was a grammarian who wrote ele- ven epigrams, which are preserved in the *Greek Anthology*;

very little is known about him except that he may have been of Spanish origin.

127   **MAURICE AUGUSTE BARRÈS** (1862–1923) was a French writer and champion of what one would regard today as right-wing political causes.

141   **GERTRUDE BELL** (1868–1926) was a British traveler, political agent, and writer who lived for many years in the Middle East; she described her experiences in classic works of travel writing such as *The Desert and the Sown.*

35, 81, 103   **EDOUARD BLONDEL** was a French writer who lived in Beirut from 1838 through 1839.

41, 46, 54, 93, 102, 125, 131   **GABRIEL CHARMES** (1850–86) was a French journalist, traveler, and specialist in foreign affairs.

65   **J. LEWIS FARLEY** (1823–85) was an Irish diplomat and banker who spent two years in Beirut as Chief Accountant for the Ottoman Bank.

ROBIN FEDDEN (1908–77) taught English literature at Cairo University. He became a writer on historic monuments including those of Syria and Lebanon as well as recording his travels in the Middle East and North Africa.

GUSTAVE FLAUBERT (1821–80) was a French Modernist novelist. He traveled in the Levant from 1849 to 1853 and recorded his impressions in his *Voyage to the Orient.*

HENRY HARRIS JESSUP (1832–1910) was a Presbyterian minister and one of the founders of the Syrian Protestant College, later the American University of Beirut. His memoirs reflect many years of sympathetic contact with the peoples of the Levant.

TITUS FLAVIUS JOSEPHUS (c. 37–100), born Yosef bin Matityahu, was a first-century Romano-Jewish historian.

ALPHONSE MARIE LOUIS DE PRAT DE LAMARTINE (1790–1869) was a French Romantic poet and politician who spent two years in the Levant in the early 1830s.

142   **T.E. LAWRENCE** "of Arabia" (1888–1935) was a British army officer who is known for having helped organize the "Arab Revolt" against Ottoman rule in the Arab lands during the First World War, immortalized in his epic *Seven Pillars of Wisdom.*

121, 139   **THE R.P. LAORTY-HADJI** (S.J.) was a French Jesuit priest who spent time in the Levant prior to 1854.

20, 23, 55   **HENRY MAUNDRELL** (1665–1701) was an Oxford academic and clergyman who wrote a detailed account of his Levantine pilgrimage in 1697.

5, 26, 37,
44, 67   **JOHN MURRAY** is a British publishing house founded in 1768. Murray's *Handbook for Travellers in Syria and Palestine* was first published in 1858 and was written by the Reverend Josiah Leslie Porter. It went through several editions.

13   **NASIR-I-KHUSRAU** (1004–1088) was a Persian poet, scholar, and traveler who visited the Levant a generation before the Crusades and recorded his experiences in an influential travel memoir, the *Safarnameh*.

GÉRARD DE NERVAL (1808–55), a French Romantic poet, did the Grand Tour in 1843 and recorded his impressions, which combine poetic color with detailed and sympathetic description.

NONNUS OF PANOPOLIS was a native of Upper Egypt who lived around 500 and composed a long epic in Greek, the *Dionysiaca*.

JOHANNES PHOCAS (fl. c. 1185), originally from Crete, was a cleric of the Eastern Orthodox Church who made the pilgrimage to the Holy Land in 1185.

REVEREND RICHARD POCOCKE (1704–65), an English clergyman, visited the Levant in 1737–41, leaving a detailed and much-praised description of his experiences.

19   **ANTOINE REGNAULT** (fl. c. 1545–75) was a self-described "bourgeois de Paris" who toured the Holy Land as a pilgrim in 1549 and published his memoirs in Lyon on his return.

71   **JEAN DE LA ROQUE** (1661–1745) was a French traveler and writer who wrote detailed descriptions of the lands and societies of the Levant and Yemen in the early eighteenth century, before Levantine travel had become commonplace.

8   **STRABO** (c. 63BC–AD24) was a Greek philosopher, historian, and, especially, geographer.

101, 134   **MARK TWAIN** (1835–1910), the pseudonym of Samuel Clemens, was a popular American writer. He went on a world tour with a large group of American pilgrims, traveling through Beirut and Lebanon on their way to the Holy Land.

DAVID URQUHART (1805–77) was a Scottish diplomat, *86, 97* writer, and (after his return from the Levant) promoter of the Turkish bath in Britain.

VISCOUNT MARIE EUGÈNE MELCHIOR DE VOGÜÉ (1848– *92* 1910) was a French diplomat, Orientalist, and writer who toured the Middle East in 1873.

C.F. VOLNEY or Constantin François de Chassebœuf, *50* comte de Volney (1757–1820) was a French writer and abolitionist who resided in Lebanon for two years, returning to France in 1785 to write up his memoirs.

WILLIAM OF TYRE (1130–86) was a prelate and chronicler *15* of the Crusader kingdom where he was born, eventually becoming Archbishop of the Crusader state of Tyre, south of Beirut.

Bibliography

d'Arvieux, Laurent, *Mémoires du Chevalier d'Arvieux, Envoyé extraordinaire du Roy à la Porte, Consul d'Alep, d'Alger, de Tripoli & d'autres Echelles du Levant,* Paris, 1735 [posthumous; Lebanese travels 1653–60].

Baedeker, Karl, *Handbook for Travellers to Palestine and Syria,* London, 1876.

Baedeker, Karl, *Handbook for Travellers to Palestine and Syria,* London, 1894.

Barbucallus, Joannes, in *The Greek Anthology,* trans. W.R. Paton, *The Loeb Classical Library* (Book 9), London, 1917.

Barrès, Maurice Auguste, *Une enquête au pays du levant,* Paris, 1923 [posthumous: voyage described in 1914].

Bell, Gertrude, *The Letters of Gertrude Bell,* New York, 1927.

Blondel, Edouard, *Deux Ans en Syrie et en Palestine* [1839–40], Paris, 1840.

Charmes, Gabriel, *Voyage en Syrie: impressions et souvenirs,* Paris, 1891 [describing visit in 1878].

Farley, J. Lewis, *Two Years in Syria,* London, 1858.

Fedden, Robin, *Syria and Lebanon,* London: John Murray, 1965.

Flaubert, Gustave, *Voyage en Orient,* in *Œuvres complètes de Gustave Flaubert: Notes de voyage,* vols. I and II, Paris: Louis Conard, 1910.

Jessup, Henry, *Fifty-three Years in Syria,* New York, 1910.

Josephus, Flavius, *Antiquities of the Jews*, trans. William Whiston, London, 1757.

de Lamartine, Alphonse, *Travels in the East*, Paris, 1839.

Lawrence, T.E., *Seven Pillars of Wisdom*, London, 1937.

Laorty-Hadji (Le R.P.), *La Syrie, La Palestine et la Judée, Pèlerinage à Jérusalem et aux Lieux Saints*, Paris, 1854.

Maundrell, Henry, *A Journey from Aleppo to Jerusalem at Easter A.D. 1697*, Oxford, 1703.

Murray's *Handbook For Travellers in Syria and Palestine*, London: John Murray, 1858.

Nasir-i-Khusrau, *Diary of a Journey through Syria and Palestine*, trans. Guy Le Strange, London: Palestine Pilgrims' Text Society, 1893.

de Nerval, Gérard, *Voyage en Orient*, Paris, 1851.

Nonnus of Panopolis, *Dionysiaca*, trans. W.H.D. Rouse, in *The Loeb Classical Library*, Cambridge and London, 1942.

Phocas, Johannes, *The Pilgrimage of Johannes Phocas to the Holy Land in the Year 1185 AD*, Palestine Pilgrims' Text Society, London, 1896.

Pococke, Richard, *A Description of the East, and Some Other Countries*, vol. II, Part 1, London, 1745.

Regnault, Antoine, *Discours du Voyage d'Outre Mer au Saint-Sépulcre de Jérusalem, et autres lieux de la terre Saincte*, Lyon, 1573 [voyage in 1548–49].

de la Roque, Jean, *Voyage de Syrie et du Mont-Liban*, Paris 1722.

Strabo, *The Geography of Strabo, Literally Translated with Notes, the First Six Books by H.G. Hamilton, Esq., the Remainder by W. Falconer, MA*, London, 1857.

Twain, Mark, *Innocents Abroad, or the New Pilgrim's Progress*, Hartford, 1871.

Urquhart, David, *The Lebanon: A History and a Diary*, 2 vols., London, 1860 [events described 1849–50].

de Vogüé, Viscount Marie Eugène Melchior, *Syrie, Palestine, Mont Athos: Voyage aux pays du passé*, Paris, 1876.

Volney, C.F., *Travels through Syria and Egypt in the years 1783, 1784, and 1785. Containing the present natural and political state of those countries, their production, arts, manufactures and commerce; with observations on the manners, customs and government of the Turks and Arabs*, translated from the French, in two volumes, London, 1787.

William of Tyre, Archbishop, *Histoire des faits et gestes dans les régions d'outremer* in *Recueil des Historiens des Croisades, Historiens occidentaux I*, Paris, 1844–95 [translated by the editor; also translated by Emily Atwater Babcock and A.C. Cross, New York, 1943]

Acknowledgments

The editor and publisher acknowledge with thanks the kind permission of Frances Fedden and Katharine Fedden to use excerpts in this book from *Syria and Lebanon* by Robin Fedden.

Illustration Sources

The illustrations in this volume are from: Adrien Bonfils: cover (c.1895), 22 (c.1882), 98 (c.1880); Jean Lauffray, "Forums et monuments de Béryte," *Bulletin du Musée de Beyrouth* VII (1944–45): 1; Nina Jidejian, *Beirut: A City of Contrast* (Beirut: Aleph, 2008): 4, 53, 96, 137; R.P. Laorty-Hadji, *La Syrie, la Palestine, et la Judée* (Paris, 1854): 11, 67, 72; Henry Sauvaire: 12 (c.1860); Henry B. Ridgaway, *The Lord's Land, a Narrative of Travels in Sinai, Arabia Petraea* (New York, 1876): 18; John Carne, *Syria, the Holy Land, Asia Minor, in a Series of Views Drawn from Nature by W.H. Bartlett, William Purser, etc.* (London, 1836): 29, 49; Otto von Ostheim: 60 (c.1860); Pascal Sébah: 84 (c.1873); anonymous: 103 (c.1890); Gérard de Martimprey: 108 (c.1890); Wikicommons: 124; Sarrafian Bros.: 130 (c.1900); T.J. Gorton 146 (1967).